THE
WYE VALLEY
WALK

Christmas 1999
from Pat

Also available
The Cotswold Way
The Dales Way
The Saxon Shore Way
The West Highland Way
The Two Moors Way
The Southern Upland Way
The Heart of England Way

RECREATIONAL PATH GUIDE

THE
WYE VALLEY
WALK

ANTHONY BURTON

Photographs by Rob Scott

Aurum Press

Ordnance Survey

First published 1998 by Aurum Press Limited,
25 Bedford Avenue, London WC1B 3AT,
in association with the Ordnance Survey.

A catalogue record for this book is available from the British Library.

ISBN 1 85410 532 9

Book design by Robert Updegraff
Printed and bound in Italy by Printer Trento Srl

Cover: *The Wye from Symonds Yat*
Title page: *The winding river seen from Merbach Hill.*

CONTENTS

Circular walks will be found on pages: 56, 72, 82, 120, 122, 136

How to use this guide

This guide is in three parts:
· The introduction, historical background to the area and advice for walkers.
· The path itself, described in seven chapters, with maps opposite each route description. This part of the guide also includes information on places of interest as well as a number of related short circular walks. Key sites are numbered in the text and on the maps to make it easy to follow the route description.
· The last part includes useful information such as local transport, accommodation, organizations involved with the path, and further reading.

The maps have been prepared by the Ordnance Survey® for this guide using 1 : 25 000 Pathfinder® and Outdoor Leisure™ maps as a base. The line of the Wye Valley Walk is shown in yellow, with the status of each section of the path – footpath or bridleway for example – shown in green underneath (see key on inside front cover). These rights of way markings also indicate the precise alignment of the path at the time of the original surveys, but in some cases the yellow line on these maps may show a route which is different from that shown by those older surveys, and in such cases walkers are recommended to follow the yellow route in this guide. Any parts of the path that may be difficult to follow on the ground are clearly highlighted in the route description, and important points to watch for are marked with letters in each chapter, both in the text and on the maps. *Some maps start on a right-hand page and continue on the left-hand page – black arrows (➞) at the edge of the maps indicate the start point.* Should there have been a need to alter the route since publication of this guide for any reason, walkers are advised to follow the waymarks or signs which have been put up on site to indicate this.

DISTANCE CHECKLIST

This list will help you in calculating the distances between places on the Wye Valley Walk, whether you are planning overnight stops, lunch stops or checking your progress. Note that these are distances between points on the walk itself and do not include diversions to hotels, villages and so forth close to the route.

Location	Approximate distance from previous location	
	miles	km
Rhayader	0	0
Newbridge	9	14.5
Builth Wells	7	11.5
Erwood Bridge	7	11
Glasbury	8.5	13.5
Hay-on-Wye	5	8.5
Bredwardine	8.5	14
Breinton	11	18
Mordiford	8	12.5
Hole-in-the-Wall	8.5	14
Kerne Bridge	8	13
Symonds Yat	8	13
Redbrook	8	12.5
Brockweir	7.5	12
Chepstow	7	11.5

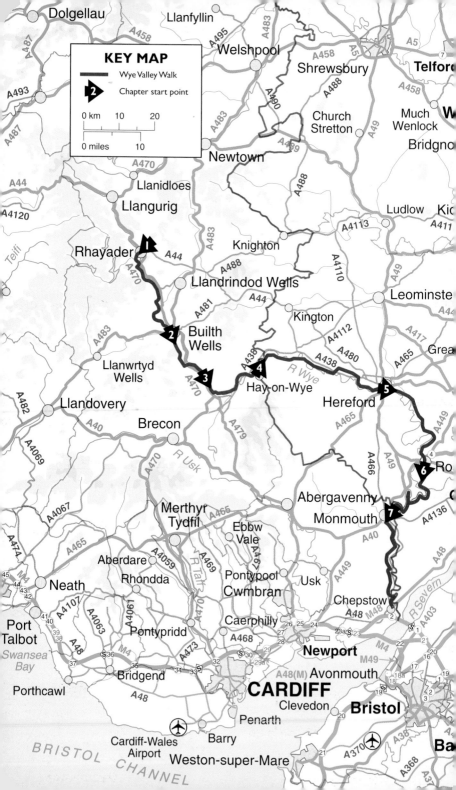

INTRODUCTION

WALKING IN THE WYE VALLEY

To some, the idea of walking a river valley might suggest a gentle amble along grassy banks, always relaxing and never strenuous. The Wye Valley Walk is not exactly like that, and to understand the nature of the walk one has to appreciate the character of the river and the geological forces that formed it.

The Wye has its origins on the slopes of Plynlimon. By the time it reaches Rhayader it has already travelled some 25 miles, gathering water from tributary streams, so that by then it has achieved a respectable size and earned the name of river. But it has not yet lost the dash and vigour of a mountain stream as it bounds over rocks and rushes down rapids. The underlying rock is Ordovician, similar to that found in Snowdonia, but here mostly buried deep, so that the hills are smoothed out rather than erupting as jagged mountain peaks. It is a landscape typical of mid-Wales, and the very name was taken from the Ordovices, ancient inhabitants of Wales, even though the rocks were formed some 500 million years ago, when animal life was confined to the sea. The river moves on into a different geological band, the old red sandstones of the Devonian period, formed a hundred million years or so later. Now the river wanders through the rich red earth carving out extravagant loops. The final section is the most dramatic of all as it reaches a limestone region, and here is something of an enigma. Geologists expect a river to carve a more or less straight path down faults in the stone, yet the Wye perversely continues to meander. The likeliest explanation seems to be that the river began by wandering over ancient rocks, and that when the newer rocks began to form the old pattern was retained, biting ever deeper on a pre-set course.

So here we have a river of constantly changing character, and a great deal of credit is due to the planners of the Wye Valley Walk for enabling us to enjoy all its varied moods and characters. Instead of sticking slavishly to the riverbank, the walk often cuts across the meanders. In the upper reaches this means taking a path over high moorland, though never too high – the walk reaches a maximum height of 390 metres (1300 feet) near the start of the walk. While at the far end, there are magnificent views down from above the limestone crags. There is no shortage of drama on the Wye Valley Walk. The scenery changes all the time, and it is difficult to imagine a greater contrast than that between the rich red earth of the agricultural land around Hereford and the rocky gorge with its ancient woodland above Tintern.

The first question to be decided is the direction in which to walk. There are three reasons for selecting Rhayader as a starting point. Firstly, it is more difficult to reach by public transport than Chepstow, and most people seem to like to get home with the minimum of fuss at the end of the walk. Secondly, as the general direction of the walk is south-westerly you are more likely to have the wind at your back. And thirdly, rivers run downhill so that you start at a height of around 650 feet (200 metres) and finish at sea level, so although the route has many ups and downs, there is still 650 feet less climbing to do.

The next question is when to travel. This is very much a matter of personal choice, for each season has its own pleasures. Winter obviously creates the greatest problems, not just with weather – and the uplands can be very bleak – but also in terms of shorter days. The author has walked the route in March, when snow was still around, and found it highly enjoyable, partly because of the great vistas in the lower valley that are closed off when the trees are in leaf. Later, in spring and early summer, there are special delights, and no one can

Apple blossom brightens the way through an orchard near Monnington-on-Wye.

The majestic nave of Hereford cathedral. As well as its architectural splendours, Hereford is famous for its chained library.

forget the brilliance of the bluebells that carpet so much of the woodland. Summer has obvious advantages, but for many autumn is the best time of all, the days are – with luck – warm, but not unbearably hot, and it is then, as the leaves begin to turn, that the woodland is at its finest. The notes for this book were taken during a walk made in September. In the end it is all down to individual preference, for this is very much an all-seasons walk.

The final question is how long to allow. It is certainly perfectly feasible for a normally fit person to do the whole walk in one week. There are hills to climb, but the ascents are never very long or particularly demanding. On the other hand, this is also a walk which encourages a slow pace, for there is so much to see along the way. The Wye valley is rich in history, and though the archaeological remains are few when one looks for the earliest traces of human activity, they are abundant once one reaches the Iron Age. There is, it seems, scarcely a promontory or hill that does not boast its fort, protected by bank or ditch. Moving forward in time, the Romans have left their marks, notably in their roads near Goodrich and Hereford. The Dark Ages are well represented by Offa's Dyke, but the richest period of all is that of the Normans. The castles that line the river are often spectacular, but they are surpassed in beauty by the abbey at Tintern, arguably the most famous of any in Britain. Wordsworth walked the hills above Tintern and felt its spiritual power:

> That blessed mood,
> In which the burthen of the mystery,
> In which the heavy and the weary weight
> Of all this unintelligible world,
> Is lightened.

Tourism and coach parties have not yet destroyed the unique atmosphere. The valley really does have something for everyone. There is the natural beauty of the scenery, side by side with the remnants of a busy industrial past.

For those who want to explore the delights to be found just a little way from the route, this book provides suggestions for circular walks and excursions. These take in the whole range of sites from ancient monuments to the impressive works of Victorian engineers, from wild scenery to charming follies. Even walkers who regard historical landmarks as little more than unwelcome intrusions into a natural world of beauty will not be disappointed in the Wye. In 1971, the southern section of the valley, from Hereford down to Chepstow, was officially designed as an Area of Outstanding Natural Beauty, and few would

The signpost for the bridleway also marks the top of the first climb of the Wye Valley

Walk on the hills above Rhayader.

quarrel with the description. In short, those who would want to extend the walk from one week to two need not worry about having enough to occupy their time.

The walk itself may not be overly demanding, but that does not mean that it can be taken lightly. Any walk that extends over a hundred miles demands respect and a certain level of physical fitness. There are a number of steep climbs and rough paths along the way, and much of the walk in the upper sections is over very exposed high ground. It is therefore important that walkers who are setting out to cover the entire route should be properly prepared. This means genuine waterproof clothing and, at the very least, stout walking shoes, though walking boots are far preferable for the support they provide over stony paths and rocky ways.

In general, there are few problems in following the path, which is waymarked throughout – by signposts carrying the emblem of a leaping salmon in the Powys section and by arrows and yellow dots elsewhere. It is never, however, advisable to rely entirely on waymarks. Anyone with experience of long-distance paths knows that they can disappear from the landscape as a result of natural accident or wilful vandalism. On one section of a walk – not the Wye Valley – the author

A visitor arrives in style at Monnington Court.

The bridge that once carried the trains of the Wye Valley Railway now carries pedestrians on the Wye Valley Walk.

found that some joker has turned half a dozen signposts round to face the wrong way! So, every walker should be prepared in case things go wrong. Although the path seldom strays very far from hamlet, village or town, there are a number of exposed sections and even the simplest walk can prove taxing when mists rise or clouds settle low over the hills. In these circumstances a map alone is not enough and a compass becomes an essential navigational aid. And even that is little use unless the walker knows how to use it correctly.

Troubles invariably come at the least appropriate moment. No one expects to have an accident, but accidents do happen, and a sprained ankle can be as debilitating as a broken limb. This can be particularly serious for solitary walkers. Those who walk alone should always make sure

The Wye at its most placid, flowing gently beneath drooping willows on the outskirt

f Hereford.

that someone knows where they are walking from and to and what time they expect to arrive. Then, if things go wrong, rescuers will find their task all the easier. A whistle is an invaluable aid in attracting attention. Minor accidents can be irritating or can develop into something altogether more serious, so a simple first-aid kit should always be carried. Plasters for blisters are a must, and an insect repellent is often needed in the middle of summer. This is not a walk fraught with danger, but a few simple precautions can ensure that a mishap does not become a tragedy.

Planning the walk is a matter of personal choice. Those who carry their own tents and equipment will enjoy the greatest freedom, able to extend the day's walking in beautiful weather, or cut it short when things turn foul. For others who prefer a comfy bed, a soak in a hot bath and someone else to do the cooking, there is no shortage of accommodation along the walk. It is, however, rather more sparse at the upper end, and booking in advance is probably a good idea. There are notes on accommodation at the end of this book.

Authors of guide books such as this invariably feel obliged to warn readers about difficulties along the way and things that can go wrong. But there is no need to get unduly worried. The Wye Valley Walk is a delight, offers few major difficulties and these precautionary notes are meant to do no more than help the walker to ensure that nothing happens to spoil the enjoyment. In the end, all an author can do is to proclaim just how splendid the Wye Valley Walk is, and to wish readers as much pleasure from it as he has received. Happy walking!

THE WORKING RIVER

Today, it is difficult to see the Wye as anything other than the centrepiece of a beautiful, rural landscape, yet for centuries it was a trading river, linking important industrial centres. Chepstow was once the major port of South Wales and, from around 1750 until the 1920s, an important shipbuilding centre. The yards began by building wooden sailing ships, brigs and brigantines, but worked on into the steamship era. There were some famous connections. Finch's provided the masts for Brunel's *Great Eastern* and in the Second World War the wharves were busy again producing sections of Mulberry Harbour. Sea-going vessels called regularly at Chepstow, and trade was carried far up river in sailing barges, notably the large Severn trows. Old wharves can still be seen at many places up river.

The most important industry depended on local resources. Until the eighteenth century, iron making depended on three basic ingredients: iron ore, charcoal as a fuel and limestone as a flux – all avail-

A pedestrian tunnel takes the Walk along the limestone cliffs on the approach to Chepstow.

The old Broomy Hill Waterworks, now preserved as a museum, complete with massive steam pumping engines.

able in the area. Iron ore has been extracted from the Forest of Dean since Roman times, and the Romans established iron works at *Ariconium*, near the walk at Weston-under-Penyard. By the sixteenth century there was a great demand for wire, which was mostly supplied from Europe. But in 1565, William Humphrey, Assay Master of the Royal Mint, obtained a patent for a new process and set up a works at Tintern, where a water wheel was used to power simple machinery to draw the hot metal through ever smaller holes. Soon blast furnaces were built nearby, and one of them survives in reasonably good condition near the walk at Coed Ithel in the woods north of Tintern.

Other metal industries depended on copper and tin, brought across the Bristol channel from Cornwall. A copper works was established at Redbrook by Swedes, 'and other foreigners', around 1690 and a century later the Redbrook Tinplate Works was established on the same site. All this activity called for new transport, and in 1812 Redbrook was linked to the iron and coal mines of the Forest of Dean by the Monmouth Railway. Horses did the work on the flat, but at Redbrook trucks were lowered down the hill by cable on an inclined plane, and the curious sloping-topped bridge can still be seen in the village. Across the river at Whitebrook, there were four or five paper mills which made, among other things, high quality white paper for the old five-pound note.

The River Wye was undoubtedly a busy and important thoroughfare for very many centuries.

WOODLAND

The Wye Valley is famous for its woods: not the dark, drab uniformity of conifer plantations, but beautiful broad-leaved woodland. The mixture is a rich one of mature oak, beech, ash, hazel, sweet chestnut, yew and more. The special qualities of these woods have been recognized by many sections being designated as nature reserves. Wyndcliff Woods were established as a reserve in 1959, for example, while Little Doward was bought by The Woodland Trust. It is not just the trees themselves that are the attraction. The forest floor is often bright with flowers – bluebells appear in profusion, along with dog's mercenry, wood anemones and wild garlic - and a rich variety of fungi. Wildlife is plentiful, including fallow deer and the tiny secretive muntjac deer. Birds, even if they cannot always be seen, can usually be heard, whether it is the rat-a-tat-tatting of a woodpecker, the hoarse cry of the pheasant or the coo-cooing of the wood

Autumn adds rich colour to the woods that flank the Wye on the approach to Symor

pigeon. And there are some even more spectacular residents. The high limestone cliffs that push out above the trees on the lower reaches of the river provide a nesting site for the spectacular pere-grine falcon.

The woodlands may have all the appeal of the natural world, but they are very far from being in a state of nature. The forests of Wyedean were being exploited by man as early as 1250. They had many different uses. In earlier times, nuts were a valuable source of food. Oak bark was a vital ingredient for tanneries set up along the river at Ross, Monmouth and Hereford. But the principal use of trees was as a source of fuel and building materials. Charcoal making was

t.

for centuries a vital part of the woodland scene. The charcoal burners worked in the forest itself: it was easier to stay close to the source of heavy wood and send away the light charcoal than it was to move the timber to another site. So pits were made in the wood, and logs of a uniform length and thickness were carefully built up into a pyramid that might contain a ton or more of wood, covered over and left to smoulder away very slowly under carefully controlled conditions. The uniform logs were supplied by coppicing. Maple, wych-elm, ash and hazel were particularly useful. If the tree is cut back to the stump, it will send up new poles that can grow as much as two inches a day. When they reach the right size, they are cut back and the process starts all over again. The typical coppiced woodland with bulky stumps sending up slender poles can be seen in many parts of these woods. Timber has, of course, many uses, from building to furniture making. The old Abbey Forge at Tintern was for many years a wood turnery and sawmill.

Throughout the woods there are signs of careful management: coppicing, boundary banks and ditches to mark out ownership, paths for pack-horses to remove the woodland products. The woods of the Wye valley are a living historical record as well as areas of natural beauty.

PICTURESQUE SCENERY

Asked to describe the attractions of a walk in the Wye valley, most people would put 'beautiful scenery' high on the list. Yet this is a comparatively modern notion. When Daniel Defoe went on his great journey round England at the beginning of the eighteenth century, he reached the Lake District and declared that 'the pleasant part of England was at an end', and a little later, Dr Johnson visited the Scottish Highlands and was 'astonished and repelled by this wide extent of hopeless sterility'. The promotion of wild scenery as a thing of delight began with the publication of just one book: William Gilpin's *Observations on the River Wye*, which first appeared in 1770.

Gilpin was a clergyman, the author of a number of dull but worthy theological tomes, before he turned to travel, and reading the Wye book today it is difficult to see why it seemed so exciting at the time. But what he was doing was proposing a whole new way of looking at scenery. Before his time an attractive scene meant a prosperous one, replete with fat cattle and rich grain. He proposed that scenery should be considered in terms of how it would look in a picture. The sort of pictures he had in mind were the fashionable romantic landscapes of the French painters Gaspard, Poussin and Claude, full of ruined castles and shattered crags. He found just such a view at Goodrich:

> A reach of the river forming a noble bay, is spread before the eye. The bank on the right is steep, and covered with wood; beyond which a bold promontory shoots out, crowned with a castle, rising among the trees. This view, which is one of the grandest on the river, I should not scruple to call *correctly picturesque.*

Gilpin had not only begun a new movement, he had given the language a new word 'picturesque'.

This simple little suspension bridge appears near the beginning of the Walk, crossing not the Wye, but its tributary the Elan.

Two of Monmouth's local heroes: Henry V holds his sceptre aloft, while the Hon. C.S. Rolls admires a model of his biplane.

Sadly for Gilpin, the world scarcely ever met his high standards, and nature failed to organize itself into just the right proportions. Even Tintern Abbey was too uniform in outline, and he longed to correct it: 'a number of gabel-ends hurt the eye with their regularity; and disgust by the vulgarity of their shape. A mallett judiciously used (but who durst use it?) might be of service in fracturing some of them.' Happily, no one did take a hammer to the abbey, but thousands came to hunt out the scenes he had described.

What was begun by Gilpin was continued by the Romantic poets, notably Wordsworth, who saw more in Tintern Abbey than simply a thing of cold stone to be represented in delicate watercolours on a sketching pad. He also felt its history and heard 'the still, sad music of humanity'. For most of us today, the Wye valley has an appeal that owes a lot to both Gilpin and the Romantics. We still see it as picturesque, but are equally conscious of the historic forces that have helped shape the landscape.

THE DEFENDED FRONTIER

The river, for much of its length, forms an obvious division between England and Wales. This natural boundary was reinforced by Offa, King of Mercia, from AD 757-796. The native Britons had been driven westward and Offa ordered the construction of a great bank and ditch to mark off the two regions. Offa's Dyke now forms the basis for another popular long-distance walk that runs close to the Wye Valley in the southern section.

What Offa began, the Normans continued, erecting their castles all along the valley. Some now survive only as grassy mounds, the mottes on which the keeps once perched.

At Hay-on-Wye both the motte and the remains of the outer court or bailey can be seen. Others have survived in almost full grandeur. Immediately after the Conquest, William FitzOsbern was created Earl of Hereford and he at once set to work building a castle on a promontory above the Wye at Chepstow as a base for an advance into the Kingdom of Gwent. The earliest surviving portion is the great tower, completed in 1072, but altered and enlarged over the years. The massive gatehouse with its guardroom and prison was built in the thirteenth century. Unusually, we know the name of the mason who built the elaborate domestic quarters and the chapel with its fine ornamental carvings. He was Master Roff, and he was paid two shillings a week for his work. With its immense curtain wall, the castle is still the dominant feature in the town.

If Chepstow has a rival for grandeur, then it is Goodrich Castle. The massive outer walls are built from the same red sandstone on which the castle rests. The perimeter defences are daunting, with a barbican set beyond the moat, surrounded by its very own secondary moat. Inside, the gaunt keep, part of the original building, looks curiously anachronistic, a square bastion of grey limestone contrasting with the curved orange red walls of the other buildings. If the overall effect is of stern defence, there is a touch of elegance to be found as well in the tall arches of the solar and the delicate tracery of the chapel windows.

Monmouth's castle has been much changed over the years, but has retained its military associations, as Great Castle House became the headquarters of the Royal Monmouthshire Engineer Militia in 1875. Far more interesting, however, is the town bridge over the River Monnow, the very last to preserve a fortified gate in the whole of Britain. It is especially appropriate that Monmouth retains such strong connections to its warlike past, for here, in 1387, was born Harry of Monmouth, later to become Britain's most famous warrior king, Henry V.

FISH AND FISHING

The Wye is known to support almost thirty different species of fish but two in particular have made the river famous, and you could hardly find a greater contrast in the fishy world than that between the salmon and the eel.

Quite when fishing with a rod began is uncertain, but the first manual on the subject appeared as early as 1496. Dame Juliana Berners was the author of *Treatyse of Fysshynge wyth an Angle*, and all the anglers who have followed her would echo these words: 'And if the angler take fysshe, surely thenne is there no man merier than he is in his spyryte.' One of the delights of fishing for the famous Wye salmon is the selection, and for the nimble-fingered the making, of the flies that will be cast to search out the fish and lure it to its doom. Gervase Markham, writing in 1597, gave his readers a list of essential ingredients:

> Fur, Feathers, Wool, Down, Silk, Worsted, Bear's Hair, Camel's Hair, Badger's Hair, Spaniel's Hair, Dog's Hair, Sheep's Wooll, Mo-hair, Cow-hair, Camlets, Furs, Hackles or Feathers of a Cock's neck or tail of several colours, Silk of all Colours, Wire and Twist, Silver Twist, Gold Twist, Silver and Gold Wyre.

He also suggested tempting the fish to the area with a delicious paste made, rather alarmingly, of 'man's fat and the fat of the thigh-bone of a heron'.

The river had its own fishing hero, Robert Pashley, who lived in a cottage close by Kerne Bridge. He was born in 1880 and between 1908 and 1947, when he hung up his rod, he had caught almost 10,000 salmon and grilse, earning himself the title of 'Wizard of Wye'. The fishermen still come to try their luck and skill against the salmon – and pay a good deal of money for the privilege, some making use of handsome little lodges, such as those that line the bank north of Builth Wells.

Fishing for salmon has never been left entirely to men with rod, line and fly who pay for the privilege. The Wye has a long history of poaching. The poacher is, in general, less fussy about how he acquires his fish, and the salmon spear was generally thought to be one of the more efficient devices. In 1932, a group of Rhayader men collected 18 illegal salmon, and had their photographs taken, faces disguised with cotton-wool beards, with the fish laid out around them. The picture appeared in the local press to the great amusement of the locals, if not of the riparian owners.

Coarse fishing is also to be had along the Wye, even if it is considered rather *infra dig* by the game-fishing fraternity. But it is during the March spring tides on the river below Tintern that the other great fishing ritual begins. Each year millions of elvers drift with the current from their far away breeding grounds in the Sargasso Sea. It seems an extraordinary journey for these creatures, scarcely more than three inches long, to make, but they ride the tides up Severn and Wye to grow in the river. The fishermen come out at night to catch the tiny creatures, considered a great delicacy by some, especially the Spanish. Armed with nets, the men light up the river with their flashlights and catch the elvers by the bucketful. This is a straightforward commercial exercise, and the main objective is a meal on the plate, not a trophy in a glass case. But even the greatest fishing writer of them all, Izaak Walton, never forgot that fishing was part of a greater pleasure. At the end of the day he and his friends would retire to the pub, where the catch was cooked and eaten and the evening ended with a jolly drink and sing-song.

> Come, we will all join together, my host and all, and sing my scholar's catch over again; and then each man drink the tother cup, and to bed; and thank God we have a dry house over our heads.

A sentiment as appropriate to the walker as the angler.

Nearing the end of the Walk the view from the Eagle's Nest, with the Severn estuar

ready in sight in the distance.

THE REVEREND FRANCIS KILVERT

The bare facts of Kilvert's life are simply told. The son of a vicar, he was himself ordained. For seven years, from 1865 to 1872, he was a curate at Clyro across the river from Hay-on-Wye, and then, after a brief period as curate to his father at Chippenham, he returned to the Wye, ending up as vicar of Bredwardine. His life was tragically short: married in 1879, he died a month later of peritonitis at the age of 39. He might have remained unknown had his diaries, written between 1870 and 1879, not been discovered and published in 1938 to 1940. They are magical volumes, overflowing with a zest for life and time and again displaying a profound love for the Wye valley and the surrounding countryside. Once one has read the diaries, it is difficult not to think of the region round Clyro and Bredwardine as Kilvert Country.

Those who have never read Kilvert might think that the journal of a Victorian parson must be dull stuff, but he was a man who delighted in life and threw himself into everything he did – sometimes almost literally. At a dance in January 1793:

> There were screams of laughter and the dance was growing quite wild. In a few minutes all order was lost, and everyone was dancing wildly and promiscuously with whoever came to hand. The dance grew wilder and wilder. Madder and madder screamed the flying fiddle bows... Oh, it was such fun.

Not much sign of the traditionally decorous vicar there.

But it is for his descriptions of the countryside and its wildlife that he will be treasured by all who have come to love the Wye valley. He was a great walker himself, out in all weathers. On one miserable winter day he arrived at the church with his moustache frozen to his beard and unable to start the service until they thawed out. Kilvert was not writing for publication, so he was able to put down impressions just as they came to him, and time and again one reads a passage and recognizes a sight or emotion as being absolutely right and true. Here, for example, is a description at the end of a beautiful passage in which he expressed his astonishment and delight at finding, when clouds cleared, that the distant hills were white with new snow. He stayed and watched.

> The great white range which had at first gleamed with an intense brilliant yellow light gradually deepened with the sky to the indescribable red tinge that snow-fields assume in sunset light, and

then the grey cold tint crept up the great slopes quenching the rosy warmth which lingered still a few minutes on the summits. Soon all was cold and grey and all that was left of the brilliant gleaming range was the dim ghostly phantom of the mountain rampart scarce distinguishable from the greying sky.

Anyone who has walked the hills in winter can vouch for the absolute accuracy of his observations. But there is more to him than that. Alongside the poetic flights stands the mundane. Kilvert wanted to share his delight and he saw a man on a carthorse whistling as he went. But Kilvert was silent – 'I thought he would probably consider me mad.' Perhaps, but his readers still find him wonderfully sane. There are worse books to put in the rucksack for a walk by the Wye than Kilvert's – but few better.

THE

WYE VALLEY

WALK

1 RHAYADER TO BUILTH WELLS

via Llanwrthwl and Newbridge-on-Wye   *15½ miles (26 km)*

The walk starts at the war memorial in the centre of Rhayader **1**. Even if one did not know that this was a market town, one could guess it from the enormous number of pubs. Go down West Street, which boasts a delightful range of buildings. First comes a shop with an elaborate terracotta façade, then a formal eighteenth-century inn, followed by the charming, weather-boarded Cwmdauddwr Arms, built a century earlier, with the police station to keep everything in order. The road comes down to the bridge over the Wye, which lies as a deep pool that overflows down through sculpted rocks, worn into fantastic shapes by the falls. Cross the bridge and continue up the main street for a short way, then turn left **A** by the public toilets down the minor road that leads past the Triangle Inn and the church.

As the town is left behind, this becomes a quiet country lane with high banks topped by hedges, the branches of which almost meet overhead. At the top of the hill, the view opens out to reveal hills covered with heather and bracken, while an obvious railway embankment can be seen to the right. This was the Mid-Wales Railway, the first sod for which was cut here on 2 September 1859 in torrential rain; it closed in 1962. It will be met many more times along the way. Where the road turns sharply to the left **B** continue straight on along the stony track, with a view of the winding Wye valley down to the left. The lower slopes of the hills are a tidy patchwork of tiny fields, while the upper slopes have been ravaged by quarries that have spilt their shattered stone down the sides. Then the view is temporarily obscured by high hedges.

Just before the obvious track of the disused railway crosses the path **C** turn left through the metal gate, passing between weather-boarded, slate-roofed barns and then, by the remains of an old railway bridge, turn left past an old quarry. The path runs beside the railway, past an old line hut, with the trees to either side forming a green tunnel. The path then slides away from the line to enter the fringe of the little wood, with a fine hazel hedge and oak trees spreading their boughs over the track. As seems to be the case with all the Wye valley woods, there is a large and energetic squirrel population, and sometimes pairs can be seen playing tag among the branches. Bird calls vary from the mellifluous blackbirds to the screeching jay and rasping rook.

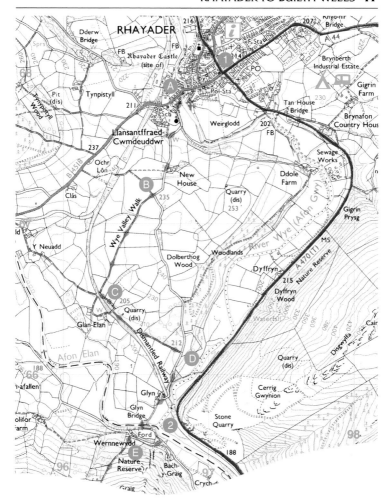

At the end of the track **D** turn right onto the road, which runs beside the river. Beyond a patch of oak woodland, turn left through the metal gate by the farm buildings onto the wide track. The track comes down to a river – not the Wye, but the Elan. Turn right along the riverbank to cross the footbridge and then turn left to meet the confluence of the two rivers **2**. An old railway viaduct crosses the Wye, which dashes along through a jumble of rocks. Turn right onto the road, which at once begins to climb up an increasingly rough hillside of bracken and scree. Where the road levels out by a smallholding **E** turn left through the wooden gate to embark upon the first steep climb of the walk. At first the narrow path is closed in by trees, then gradually emerges into the open where heather and foxgloves add colour to the bracken. Near the top is a small farm, enjoying a wonderful view back down over Rhayader and the narrow, shiny ribbon of the river. The path passes a conifer plantation and another lonely farm and then finally begins to level out as it reaches a broad expanse of heather-covered moorland. At the very top **F** there is a junction of tracks by a signpost, which marks the start of the circular walk to the Elan Reservoir (p.56).

Turn left onto a track which affords wide views of the bluff hills and the Wye valley. Go through the farmyard past an old quarry, and as the track goes downhill there are constantly changing perspectives. In the valley down to the right there is an extraordinary pattern of

The official start of the Walk in the centre of Rhayader.

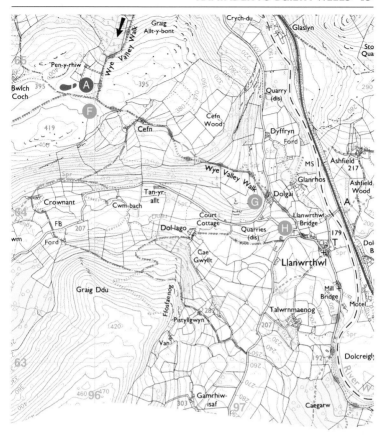

fields of all shapes and sizes, like a complex jigsaw. At the road **G** turn left and then, at the bottom of the hill, turn sharply back to the right onto a track running between stone walls, and overhung by trees. The path digs ever deeper into the hillside until the trees close up overhead; this green tunnel leads down to Llanwrthwl. At the bottom of the track **H** turn left and left again onto the road. Turn right by the little church which has its bell hung in a frame by the door. The Walk now follows a quiet lane by the river, between banks and hedgerows with good blackberrying in season. A great rounded hill looms ahead, but this time the Walk will go round not over it. At the edge of the village is a very plain chapel with some very ornate tombstones around it. Woodland soon surrounds the road – broad-leaved to one side, conifer the other – and although there are only glimpses of the Wye it is a permanent, noisy presence of rushing water.

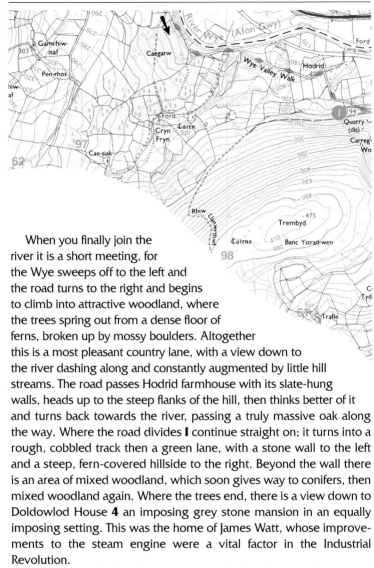

When you finally join the river it is a short meeting, for the Wye sweeps off to the left and the road turns to the right and begins to climb into attractive woodland, where the trees spring out from a dense floor of ferns, broken up by mossy boulders. Altogether this is a most pleasant country lane, with a view down to the river dashing along and constantly augmented by little hill streams. The road passes Hodrid farmhouse with its slate-hung walls, heads up to the steep flanks of the hill, then thinks better of it and turns back towards the river, passing a truly massive oak along the way. Where the road divides **I** continue straight on; it turns into a rough, cobbled track then a green lane, with a stone wall to the left and a steep, fern-covered hillside to the right. Beyond the wall there is an area of mixed woodland, which soon gives way to conifers, then mixed woodland again. Where the trees end, there is a view down to Doldowlod House **4** an imposing grey stone mansion in an equally imposing setting. This was the home of James Watt, whose improvements to the steam engine were a vital factor in the Industrial Revolution.

Where the track divides by the next patch of conifers **J** keep straight on along the line of the wall as the track starts coming down the hill past rocky outcrops. The view soon opens up again to a gentle valley scene, with the line of the old railway still clearly visible beside the river, and a backdrop of wooded hills. Passing through a gate, the Walk continues beside another wood, this time containing noble beech trees where beech nuts provide a crunchy path beneath

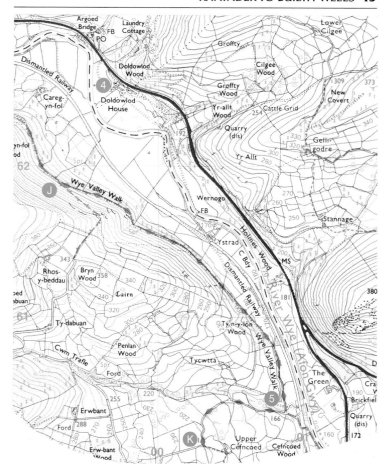

the branches. Eventually the valley floor is reached as the track runs between hedges, with the Wye tantalizingly just out of sight. It becomes a surfaced road, and there is another reminder of the Watt family: a little stone bridge, built 'at the expense of James Watt also Thomas Price' **5**. The surfaced road is now followed round to the right, once again as a quiet lane with hedgerows brightened by bramble and honeysuckle. It then heads back uphill as though the Walk is perversely trying to avoid the Wye. It does, however, offer an attractive landscape of meadows and woods, with a colourful border of wayside flowers.

At the top of the hill where the road turns sharp right **K** continue straight on over the stile to follow the line of the fence down to a footbridge over a stream. Topping a rise, look for a stile in the fence on the left. The path now goes round to the right to another footbridge. Go up the wooden steps, and turn left to follow the line of the stream. As the stream bears away to the left, go straight on to the next stile. Continue on along the fence until two stiles are reached **L** and cross the one to the left. The path leads on to a patch of conifers, and continues round the right hand side until a house is reached. Turn right into the field with the hedge on the left, cross another stile, and then look out for a stile hidden away in the corner of the next field. The path now continues over a series of stiles by the fence and hedge to the left, until they end, when it carries straight on towards the wood opposite. Once across the little bridge, go through the wood and carry straight on in the same direction to the road **M** and turn left.

This is another pleasant, tree-shaded road. The appearance of a lodge marks the start of an area of parkland, and a suitably grand,

The infant Wye dashing over a rocky bed as it bustles down through the trees near Llanwrthwl.

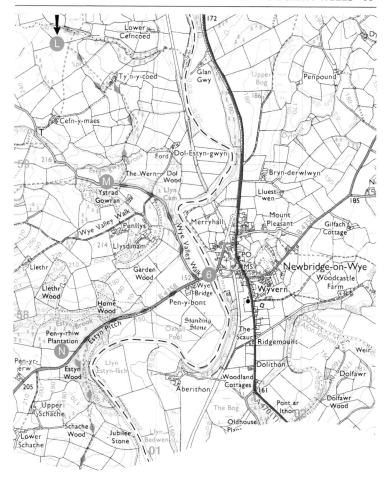

bow-fronted house duly comes into view on the right. The road comes down to the minor road. Those who wish to visit Newbridge-on-Wye for refreshment or shopping should turn left to cross the bridge **6** but those wishing to continue along the Walk must turn to the right. The road is quite busy but has wide grass verges. It runs uphill, with woodland appearing on both sides. At the top **N** turn left to cross a stile and take a path through the wood, which is mainly conifer with a sprinkling of birch. The path wanders somewhat through the trees to a stile and then heads diagonally uphill to another stile next to the iron gate in the far corner. Continue, keeping the fence on the right on this very airy part of the Walk with views in every direction. After two more fields,

Mist fills the river valley while the hills above Newbridge-on-Wye glow in the wint

...nshine.

head diagonally left, as indicated by a finger post and a marker post, to a footbridge across the stream. Continue beside the fence to a field of rough pasture which you leave by a metal gate. Continue straight on, ignoring the more obvious track that turns away to the left. At the next field look for a stile by a prominent tree in the hedge opposite. This is all delightful walking over grassy fields that eventually reaches a wood that is followed down to the road **O**.

Turn left at the road, and at the edge of the wood by the entrance to the house, Trederwen, turn right over the stile to take the path through the woods and head off towards the farm buildings. The path twists round the barns through three metal gates and then continues on, with a wire fence to the left. The field narrows and the path then follows the edge of the wood. At a large oak turn right to cross the bridge over the stream, then cross the stile and head uphill with the house on your left. The Wye comes into view and, after climbing a little, you turn left for the path along the bank **P**. For the next few miles, the Wye Valley Walk will live up to its name.

The path is a wandering, narrow affair running just inside the strip of woodland, with fields to one side and only occasional glimpses of the river itself. The bank on the left falls almost sheer to the water's edge and the route wriggles and jiggles its way through the trees before finally coming down to the riverside. The Wye has grown a good deal since it was last seen, and now gurgles and splashes over rocks and spreads out into shallows, where long green fronds of weed wave gently in the current, before widening again so that trees are seen as motionless reflections in the calm waters. Here nothing disturbs the peace, apart from the occasional spreading ripples as a fish rises to take a luckless fly. The river's mood changes constantly and it is soon splashing down again over a series of rocky ledges, which provide entertaining water chutes for the local mallards.

The path, sometimes diving into woods, sometimes out in the open, never strays far from the bank. Pass in front of a rather grand fishing lodge – here I saw a heron perched on the private jetty, enjoying the expensive fishing for free. The path follows the lodge approach road for a while, but at the top of a little hill, where the surfaced drive sweeps round to the right, carry straight on over a stile. The field-side path soon leads back to the river bank.

Fern and fir creep down to the Wye and its banks become miniature cliffs of stone. The next prominent feature is an impressive iron viaduct **7** with a tall central pier rising from the riverbed. This time, the railway is still in use, carrying the line from Craven Arms to Carmarthen Bay. The path passes underneath and is then forced up

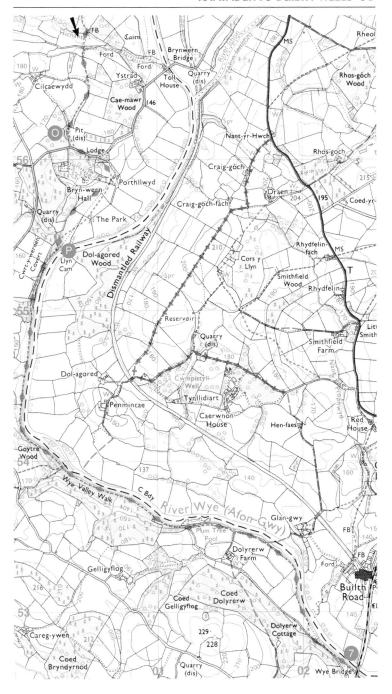

on to higher ground for another meandering woodland tour before returning again to the river's edge. It arrives in time to catch the Wye in a dramatic mood, plunging through a succession of falls. After that the houses on the outskirts of Builth Wells come into view. The walk briefly turns away from the Wye to cross the River Irfon **Q** but immediately returns. On the final approach to the town rough fields and woods give way to a municipal park, with extravagant wrought-iron gates, a bowling green, sports area and playground, while an avenue of trees turns the walk into a processional way that ends at the road leading up to the Wye Bridge **8**.

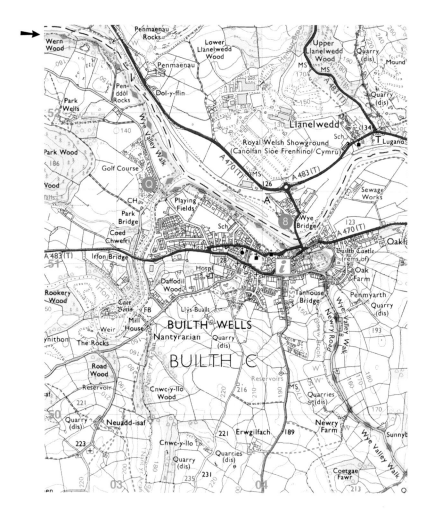

The view from Pant-y-llyn hill, looking down over the Wye near Builth Wells.

The beautiful Elan runs alongside part of the circular walk to the Elan reservoirs.

CIRCULAR WALK TO ELAN RESERVOIRS

7½ miles (12 km)

The route begins at the top of the climb up from Rhayader **A**, (see page 41), where tracks meet at the top of the hill. From the Wye Valley Walk turn right onto the bridleway, a broad track through the heather. The view down to the left is of a deep valley scooped out of the rounded hills. Continue on this track, ignoring a second track that turns sharply back on the right, towards a rocky knoll, where gorse blazes through the heather. From here there is a superb view of range upon range of hills stretching, one behind the other, to distant horizons. Just before the top of the rise, a footpath crosses the bridleway **B**. Turn right onto the path which heads uphill through a broken landscape of rocky out-crops. Go through a metal gate, with a new conifer plantation on the left. The track now becomes clearer as it passes through a little oak wood and zigzags down through the fields. It passes an attractive farm and heads down past another wood to go through an immense hairpin bend before joining the road **C**.

Turn left at the road. This is a quiet lane running between hedges and patches of woodland dominated by immense beeches. Craggy hillsides close in as the valley narrows. Where the road divides **D** turn right and follow the road through Elan Village, very much an estate village for the waterworks staff, with neat stone villas separated from the River Elan by smooth lawns dotted with fine ornamental trees, while the road itself passes through an avenue of horse chestnuts. Follow the road round to the right to cross the river for the Elan Valley Visitor Centre and picnic area **3,** dominated by the huge stone dam. Work began on constructing the reservoirs to supply water for Birmingham in 1892. This area had rows of huts that provided accommodation for the navvies and workshops, one of which has now become the Visitor Centre exhibition and café. As a reminder of the days when this was a wild river enjoyed by romantics there is a statue of Prometheus Unbound, a tribute to the area's most famous visitor, Shelley.

Go past the Centre to cross the river by the footbridge below the dam, then turn back along the river on the path that goes gently uphill through woods of sessile oaks. By a picnic area **E** continue on the upper track that doubles back through mixed woodland to reach

the top of the dam. The walk now continues along the edge of the reservoir, a wild landscape of crags and scree. The path moves gradually away from the water's edge, waymarked by yellow arrows. Where a dense conifer plantation appears up ahead **F** the path swings away from the reservoir to climb uphill beside a little rocky gorge. After a steep climb, the path divides **G**. Keep to the left past the little wood and up the hill, with superb views back over the succession of reservoirs. The path becomes a grassy track, but near the top of the hill is worn down to the bedrock. A metal gate leads into an RSPB Nature Reserve and the path arcs downhill to the road **H**. Turn right onto the road, which is at first lined with gorse before anachronistic dwarf conifers announce the arrival of houses **I**. Turn left onto the bridleway which slips up past the wood on the left and continues on with another wood on the right, to
emerge back on the high moorland.
You now walk straight on
back to the start.

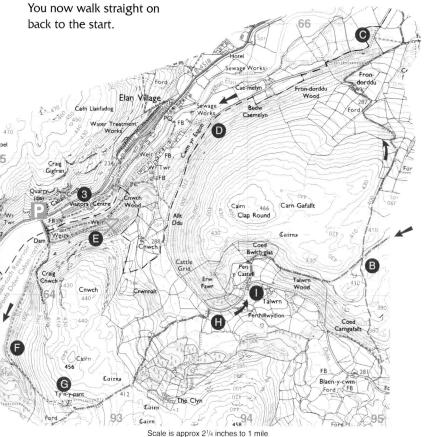

Scale is approx 2¼ inches to 1 mile

Sessile oaks dominate the hillside above the River Elan as the circular walk passes

through the Carn Gafallt Nature Reserve.

2 BUILTH WELLS TO LLANSTEPHAN BRIDGE

via Erwood Bridge   *9 miles (14.5 km)*

This is a comparatively short leg, but can be extended by a circular walk to explore the Aberedw Rocks (see page 72). On joining the road at Builth Wells, turn left towards the bridge **8**, a handsome Georgian structure with six low, stone arches. On reaching the bridge turn right and then go on up the alleyway beside The Lion Hotel, signposted to Builth Castle **9**, then turn left into another alley behind the hotel. Once across the stile you come to a classic Norman motte and bailey fortress, of which only the earthworks now remain. Beyond the outer wall is the courtyard, or bailey, from the centre of which the tall mound or motte rises up. Built around 1100, the outer earthworks would have been palisaded and later walled and the keep would have stood on the motte. Follow the path round the bailey and leave the castle site by the stile near the bungalow. Turn right onto the road that continues to circle the castle, then left along Newry Road **A**.

Sheep on the path near Twmpath.

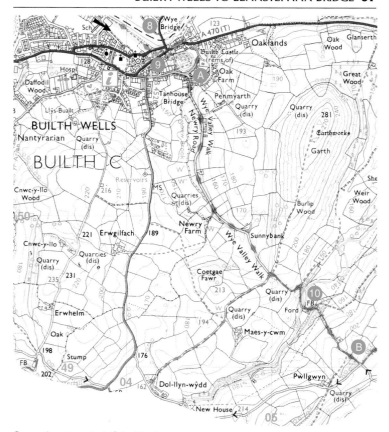

Soon the town is left behind
and the lane climbs gently up through
farmland. Continue up the road, ignoring the turning off by Newry
Cottage and a second turning by a stile. The road starts to go downhill
past tall, hazel hedges, but with a view of high hills up ahead.
Eventually the view opens out to the right to reveal a deep, wooded
valley. The road swoops down through a hairpin bend, with a wood to
the left and a glimpse of a stream at the foot of the hill. At the stream
10 there is a ford for vehicles and a footbridge for walkers. Beyond the
stream the lane becomes a grassy track that heads uphill beside the
wood. As it climbs, it bites deeper into the ground and becomes
steadily rougher and stonier, in places worn right down to the bedrock.
It is quite tough going, but very attractive with a canopy of trees pro-
viding shade.

At the top of the hill **B** the path meets a road but immediately turns
away from it onto the track to the left. The effort of the climb is

rewarded by a fine view over the hills. Near the top of the hill by a metal gate **C** turn right onto a footpath running between a fence and a hedge and passing between fields grazed by sheep while still offering magnificent views; it leads down to the road again. This time cross straight over to continue uphill on the track opposite. Gradually the little fields that cover the lower slopes are left behind and coarser, tussocky grassland takes over. Where the farm track swings round to the right **D** continue straight on along the rougher track and go through the metal gate. The underlying rock appears stratified, like a stack of plates. On reaching the top of the hill, the farm comes into view over to the right and here the few trees that survive have been stunted and bent by the wind.

Follow the track round to the right past gorse bushes; once through the gate by the little knoll you emerge onto the open hillside. Follow the track round to the left, signposted as a bridleway. This now appears as a section of superb walking on a grassy track that follows the border between the fields to the left and the rough hillside to the right. The views are immense, buzzards soar overhead, while the local sheep seem to regard every passing walker as a shepherd, so that soon one finds oneself inadvertently driving a quite considerable flock along the path up ahead. There is a temporary incursion into the

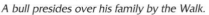

A bull presides over his family by the Walk.

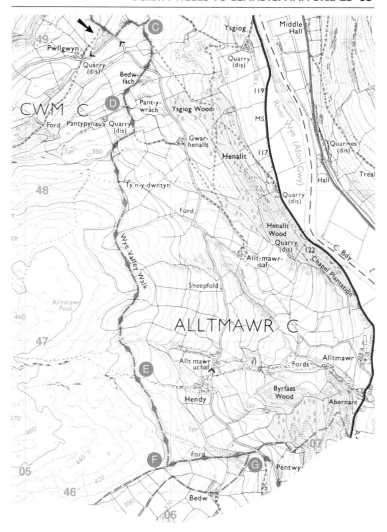

fields, before the path continues along the same line with a signpost up ahead as a marker. Leaving the fields again there is more excellent walking on springy turf through banks of heather, broken up by little crags. The way dips down to cross a small stream **E** and then continues on towards a direction post on the horizon, beyond which the route is again very clear as a broad grassy track through bracken. Continue straight on over a grassy crosstrack to the wire fence at the edge of the farmland **F**. Turn left onto the bridleway that begins heading down to the valley floor. At the road **G** turn right.

A simple footbridge across a stream, as the Walk twists through the hills on the w

Erwood.

An old saw-bench rusted to the colour of the bracken on the hillside above the fields.

At first the road runs downhill past mixed woodland, but once the woods clear there are views of the Wye and the craggy hillside beyond it. Just beyond the entrance to a house, Brynhaul **H**, turn left onto the grass and take the path that goes straight downhill avoiding the extravagant curves of the road. Where the road is rejoined, the descent steepens and it comes down to a bustling little stream and a ford. Cross this stream on the footbridge **I** and turn immediately left onto the grassy track that runs beside the stream. This path almost immediately divides and you take the path going slightly uphill to the right beside the fence. At the top of the rise it continues straight on beside the patch of woodland which spreads branches low overhead. At the little rock outcrop, cross a stile and head uphill towards the bracken. This is quite a steep little climb and it can seem mildly irritating, having almost got down to the river, to be panting up away from it again. But once the view opens up you can see what you have been spared, for a busy main road runs right down beside the Wye. A marker post indicates the line to follow and the path eventually arrives at a road.

Turn left, **J** onto the road, which soon begins a steep twisting descent through a rock-strewn landscape. At the foot of the hill, cross over the main road and Erwood Bridge, below which the river runs dark and deep in a narrow channel between rock ledges. Once across the bridge turn left onto the surfaced path, cross the stile and continue on the grass track that leads to the picnic area by Erwood Station **11**. This is the start of the circular walk to Aberedw Rocks (see page 72).

From the station, double back along the old railway line, which, beyond the cattle grid, has been transformed into a surfaced road. It now runs more or less straight and level for over two miles, but is by no means dull as there are excellent views all along the way. It passes below the shapely hill of Twyn y Garth and then crosses a deep, wooded cleft using the original railway bridge. Turn right over another old railway bridge on the road signposted to the A470 and cross the Llanstephan suspension bridge **13** which looks like a foot-bridge, but which in fact carries cars as well – but not at the same time, as there simply is not room. Down below, the Wye bounces down a set of rapids in fine style.

The narrow bridge at Llanstephan which, narrow as it is, does carry motor vehicles as well as walkers.

Aberedw Rocks: the circular walk follows a path round the foot of the crags befo

...mbing back up the hill.

CIRCULAR WALK TO ABEREDW ROCKS

6 miles (10 km)

The walk begins at the old Erwood Station **A**. This is still the same line encountered at Rhayader, but here the buildings have been retained, an old locomotive stands in what were once sidings and a carriage by the platform acts as a woodstore. The former waiting room has craft work for sale and a small café. Go through the wooden gate opposite the station buildings and turn right to follow the riverside walk beside the old trackbed – and what a delight this line must have been when trains still ran, with the Wye to one side and a dramatic rocky hillside to the other. The path leads down through mixed woodland with large clumps of rhododendra, the river calms down, and the path turns right **B** up a little flight of wooden steps. Leave the woods by the stile to cross the field, heading for a prominent tree, then turning right by the telegraph pole towards the metal gate by the road **C**.

At the road, turn right to pass through the abutments of the former railway bridge and immediately beyond the cattle grid turn left onto a minor road **D**. This is a narrow road that snakes uphill past bracken covered slopes. Shortly after passing a little wood **E** turn left onto the broad stony track, then immediately left again onto the grassy track heading back at an angle, with a view across to the Wye Valley Walk. At the top of the rise, continue uphill on the wide green track beside the fence. This reaches a plateau and the path continues straight on along the same line as the fence ends. At a crossing of tracks **F** the crags of the Aberedw Rocks break through the hill.

At this point, those who feel that they have seen enough can cut short the walk by following the instructions that pick up at point **F** below and turning back down the far side of the field to **K**. The full walk is continued by taking the path that zigzags down towards the foot of the crags. Just before the boundary stone that can be seen to the left of the path, turn right on to the narrow path through the bracken that passes beneath the impressive range of rocks. They all have a slight tilt as though a giant has leaned against them and shoved them sideways. The path stays at a high level and eventually turns in to cross a scattering of scree to reach the foot of the rocks beside a deep valley. Follow the track round the face of the crags to emerge in a little natural amphitheatre **12** almost ringed by rock faces.

From here follow the path beside the fence to a ruined farm **G**. Cross the stile, then take the rutted track away from the gate. Where the track divides go straight on, with the rocky knoll to the right. Continue in the same direction along the broader stony track. Then, as that turns away to the left **H**, carry straight on along the grassy track that follows the rim of an attractive little valley. Shortly after passing under the power cables, turn right onto the broad track **I**. After a short, stiff climb to a track junction **J** turn right, and follow this track back to point **F** above the rocks. Turn left and retrace your steps towards the field, but now turn left again to take the path, this time with the field to the right. Continue through the metal gate and take the path down to the farm cottage **K**. Continue on in the same direction down the surfaced road which leads on to the little plain church with a squat, fortress-like tower at Llandeilo Graban. Keep straight on at the crossroads after which the road dips steeply down into a little valley only to climb just as steeply back up the other side. At the road junction **L** turn right on the road signposted to Erwood, which descends very steeply through even more extravagant bends. At the next road junction **M** turn right to return to the station.

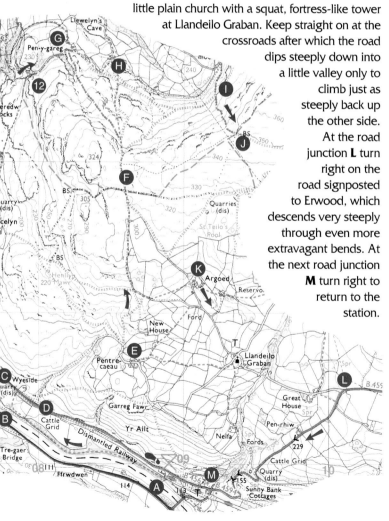

3 LLANSTEPHAN BRIDGE TO HAY-ON-WYE

via Glasbury   *11 miles (17.5 km)*

Once over the bridge **13** turn left for a short walk down the busy main road which fortunately has wide grass verges. On the right, standing next to the old road bridge is handsome, redbrick Trericket Mill, now converted into housing. Cross the stream and turn left **A** over a stile to follow the brook down to the river's edge. There is now a long stretch of peaceful and very appealing riverside walking to enjoy. Turn right to follow the Wye downstream. At first it is in a dashing mood, but the river never keeps to one phase for long, and soon the gurgles subside and it becomes a pellucid, seemingly almost motionless stream. The scenery is equally varied with rich farmland on the valley floor, overlooked by rugged hills. Closer at hand there are the riverside trees, massive beech and oak whose great roots have often been exposed by bank erosion. Across the fields there is a view of a very grand house, Llangoed Castle **14**. The seventeenth-century original was largely rebuilt by that most romantic of architects, Clough Williams-Ellis. There is a temporary diversion round a little wood, but soon the river is rejoined. Here great flat rock pavements jut out from the bank, forcing the river into a dark brown whirl of activity.

The colourfully welcoming Bridgend Inn, Boughrood.

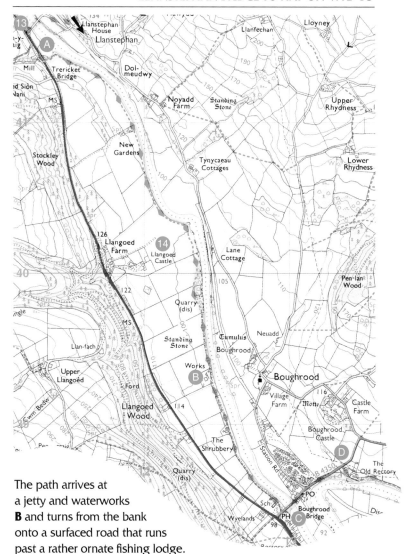

The path arrives at
a jetty and waterworks
B and turns from the bank
onto a surfaced road that runs
past a rather ornate fishing lodge.
At the road **C** turn left to cross Boughrood
Bridge: an interesting little spot this, with The Boat Inn and its riverside
garden, the old toll house and the bridge itself, a solid stone affair
topped with elegant cast-iron lamps.

Continue on up the road, while the river does a disappearing act,
shortly to reappear after completing a U-turn. After the river is rejoined,
look out for a stile in the hedge on the right **D**, cross it and take the path
down to the riverbank. This is a narrow track which, after fighting with

the dense undergrowth for a while, gives up the struggle and climbs a short flight of steps for an easier line at a higher level. Trees largely keep the river out of view, but from the sounds it is enjoying one of its busy periods. The path leaves the wood and crosses a bracken-covered stretch of land and now the river swings away. The Walk emerges into a more open area of fields, and the line of the fence is followed to a stile hidden away in a corner. The path goes along the edge of the field and there is a fine prospect of the Black Mountains up ahead. The Walk continues down a green lane, bordered by a high thickset hedge and fence, that leads down to a little village green with whitewashed cottages **E**.

Turn right onto the road, passing a farm with an imposing, buttressed barn, then as the road turns left carry straight on through the wooden gate to follow a track running between hedges. The walking now is very different from anything previously met along the way. The river winds through a wide, flat plain and the rough pasture gives way to mostly arable land. As a result, route directions can sound complex, as the path hops backwards and forwards between hedges and fences, but navigation presents no real problems on the ground.

Cross a section of open fields and continue, keeping the hedge to your left. Pass a line of tall hawthorns, and leave the next field by a wooden gate immediately beyond the line of trees.

The path now heads off to a gate behind a ruined stone building. Leave the field by the wooden gate and turn left onto the obvious track that ends at four metal gates. Take the one that opens onto a broad track, running between a fence and a hedge. Emerging from the lane, continue straight on along the line of the hedge. The way now basically continues in the same direction, passing briefly through a little wood, and carrying on towards a farm. The spire of Glasbury church can now be seen. When you come round the farm driveway, the river comes back in view, but now its character has changed as it swings gently along between low sandy banks. The track heads off across the grass to Glasbury **15**.

At the roadway, turn right and follow the road round past the hotel , then continue straight on at the road junction. Cross the road just before the bridge and cross a stile to join the riverside path. There is a meagre trickle of water, with the main flow passing the other side of a low, gravel island. The broad, placid waters prove more attractive to swans than the dancing rapids further

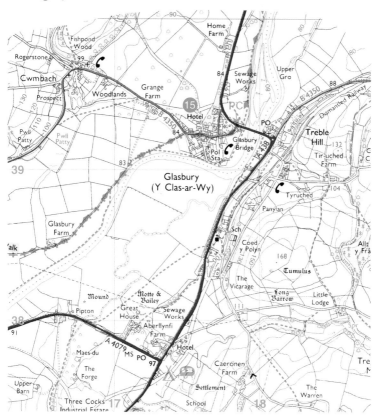

Weeds wave in the shallows and the water splashes over the rocks as the river broadens out near Hay-on-Wye.

upstream. The path briefly takes on a rather unfriendly character, narrowly squeezed between barbed wire fences. Beyond a kissing gate, the path turns away from the river towards a finger post that can just be made out in front of a patch of woodland. Cross the surfaced track and go straight down to the road **F**.

At the road turn right – there is a turning off to the left for anyone wishing to visit the little eighteenth-century Maesyronnen Chapel. This is a busy road, and even though there are wide verges, it is a relief to turn off to the left at the next road junction **G** up the lane marked 'No Through Road'. Follow this road round to the right behind a rather grand white house and continue along the track that runs past farmhouse and barns. At this point **H** leave the farm track and continue on the footpath beside the fence. There is a view down to the river, which is going through a vast meander, before the path dives into a tangle of bracken and scrub. It soon becomes a pleasant woodland amble – far preferable to the fume-ridden road down below. Emerging from the wood, keep straight on towards the iron gate between the houses **I**. Turn right onto the road for the little village of Llowes. The church **16** is an ancient foundation and makes an impressive sight with its tall crenellated tower, but much of its present appearance is due to enthusiastic Victorian restorers. The churchyard contains a little sundial dedicated to Francis Kilvert and the immense cross of St Meilig, carved some 1300 years ago. Continue down the village street, passing an attractive cottage with an old stone slate roof to return, somewhat unwillingly, to rejoin the road.

Turn left at the road by the Radnor Arms. There is a consolation prize for having to rejoin the traffic in the form of Llowes Court **17**, a wonderful old house with narrow, mullioned windows and immense external chimneys. Carry on to a lay-by with an old milestone opposite, and turn onto the footpath running parallel to the road **J**.

Cross a stile, take the path down to the river bank and follow this downstream. The river here is very broad and shallow, a fact perfectly demonstrated by a swan that suddenly stopped swimming and simply stood up in the middle.

The path stays close to the riverbank, but the water is soon lost from sight behind a fringe of trees. There are compensations in the profusion of wayside flowers on the verge between the fields and the path, ranging from tall foxgloves to tiny scarlet pimpernels. As the trees open out there are more chances to enjoy the river scenery until, just beyond a neat little fishing lodge, the Wye goes off on one of its long detours, starting with a sudden rush of rapids. At this point **K** the path turns left round the edge of the field, and then right across a footbridge. Once over the bridge, turn diagonally right to a stile and take the little path that goes uphill through scrubby woodland. A high stone wall appears beside the path and there is a good view down to the rushing Wye. At the top of the hill turn left to the stile and Hay-on-Wye appears up ahead, its castle still dominating the town from the top of the hill. Follow the path round the edge of the field to the road. The circular walk to Clyro starts here (see page 82). For the main Walk turn right to cross the bridge into the town.

The clock tower in the centre of Hay-on-Wye, a town famous for its profusion of bookshops.

CIRCULAR WALK TO CLYRO

3 miles (4.5 km)

This is a short walk, of particular interest to lovers of Kilvert, visiting his beloved Clyro and following the paths he often trod. It begins at the point **A** where the main Wye Valley Walk meets the B4351. Turn left up this road and take the first turning on the right **B** onto the single track road. The road swings round to the left and becomes a quiet lane, bordered by hedges. The surroundings are much as they were in Kilvert's day. By then the pattern of irregular fields broken up by clumps of woodland and dotted with farms was already set. There is a gentle swell of hills and the hedgerows are enlivened by the rustle and twitter of birds.

After a little over half a mile, look out for a stile by an iron gate **C**. Cross the stile and head off on a slight angle to the right, going downhill. Once through the screen of trees and over the brow of the hill, head for a second stile which can be seen at the bottom of the valley. The walk now follows the line of the fence on the right, through fields full of little dips and hollows. Once over the next stile, carry on, leaving the old stone building to the right. The right of way now follows a somewhat bizzare route.

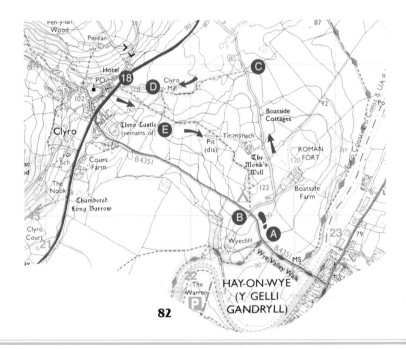

Old cottages opposite the church in Clyro.

Head for a marker post on top of the little hill **D**. At this point turn sharp left towards the end of the hedgerow **E**, and then right along the wire fence towards Clyro. The path goes round the foot of the little hill, with the scant remains of Clyro Castle on the top of it. Head for the two tall trees in front of the houses to the right of the church, leave the field by the stile, and turn left. Cross the main road to go into the village.

Immediately on the right is Ashbrook **18** the very attractive house where Kilvert had his lodgings, which is now open to the public as the Kilvert Gallery. Continue on to the church past a delightful row of old cottages. The church was built in the twelfth century, but largely rebuilt in 1853, shortly before Kilvert arrived. The most interesting features are the pews – the grander ones with doors, numbered; the less grand, doorless and lettered. There is a memorial to Kilvert and to Richard Venables, father of the vicar Kilvert served as curate. The old vicarage is on the road near the church. Much of the old village survives, but there is a good deal of new development as well.

Retrace your steps to the hedgerow **E** but instead of turning off continue straight on with the fence to the left and a panorama of hills to enjoy up ahead. At the metal gate, where the fence turns away to the left, continue straight on to a stile beside more metal gates. Go straight across the next field past a marker post to another stile. Fields are now crossed by a series of stiles until the field before the camp site is reached. Here the path goes round the edge of the field and down to the road for the return to the start.

4 HAY-ON-WYE TO HEREFORD

via Bredwardine and Byford   *25 miles (40 km)*

Cross the bridge to go into Hay-on-Wye, a town well worth exploring if only for its famously large number of bookshops, both new and secondhand. The main Walk, however, largely misses the town out altogether. Once over the bridge **A** turn left onto the footpath that leads down to the riverside path overhung by a grand old horse chestnut. Where the way is blocked up ahead, turn right up the lane by the brick houses, cross straight over the road and go up the stone steps and across the stile to take the footpath signposted to Black Lion Green. Continue on to cross another stile and join the road between the cottages. Just beyond the houses with dormer windows **B** turn sharp left onto the path going downhill. Cross the stream and the modest footbridge takes you out of Wales and into England. Head across the field on a diagonal away from the dip on the left, and another stile will be seen among the trees. Cross this stile and turn left to the simple stone slab bridge, and once over that turn right. At the top of the slope, take the stile to the right of the house, and continue up the lane for a short way until it turns sharp right **C**, then go straight on along the footpath. The hedge to the right has a rich mixture of species – hawthorn, blackthorn, elder and hazel, brightened with dog roses.

You are now on a pleasant, easily followed footpath, crossing the fields on a succession of stiles. There are patches of woodland and a smattering of individual trees, mainly oak but with the occasional proud fir, all suggestive of formal parkland. This is soon confirmed when the path crosses a drive **19** with an avenue of oak and a lodge over to the left by the road. Once past the avenue turn slightly to the right and head for the stile by the metal gate. Beyond this the park gives way to farmland, with the path running along the top of a field of crops and past an area of rough grass and saplings. This section of the way ends at a golf course **20**.

Set off across the course in the direction shown by a yellow arrow and heading towards a marker post by a clump of newly planted trees. The path now runs round the edge of the course, first beside the rough grass and then alongside the trees. Over to the right, the ornate Summerhill Tower can be seen poking up, which is in fact nothing more than a heavily disguised water tower. At the edge of the course

The steep path that climbs Merbach Hill.

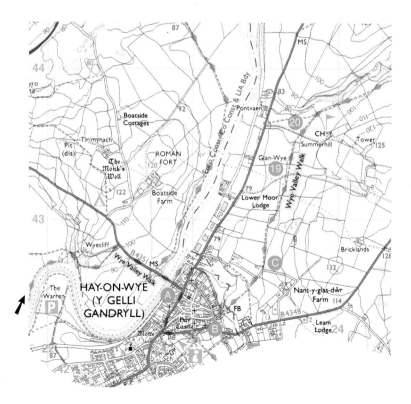

Having reached the top of Merbach Hill, walkers enjoy superb views out over the Wye valley.

turn off at an angle away from the fourth green to a marker post and a stile beyond **D**.Head straight across the rough pasture to the stream and turn right to follow it past a pool and a small cascade, and cross over the footbridge. From the bridge, take the obvious farm track to a stile by an iron gate and cross the next field, with the little brook wandering along on the right. This lovely peaceful valley walk ends at the cluster of buildings at Priory Farm up ahead **21**. It is not the no-nonsense farmhouse that attracts attention so much as the magnificent barns, one of which has a wonderful contrast of textures, combining stone walls, weather-boarding and stone slate roof. There was a Cluniac Priory, founded near Clifford in 1130, and this was part of the estate: depressions in the ground to the east of the farm are former fishponds.

At the road, turn left and almost immediately right on the path by the tall hedge. Where the track divides **E** carry straight on past two contrasting houses, an old stone cottage and a corrugated iron bungalow. Head across the field towards the little lane at the right of the row of houses to join the road. Carry on straight up the road opposite, signposted to Clifford and Whitney-on-Wye. At the road junction **F** turn right past the very plain Methodist Chapel of 1827, and go on to a little hamlet of houses, scattered round a small green **22**. One notable old house with a hipped roof has an absolutely massive chimney. Turn left onto the rough track, with a view down to the flat river valley and the distant hills. The route continues as a little footpath heading downhill following the line of a hedge, crossing a little brook and eventually reaching another road. It is very evident that the walk is entering a more prosperous farming area than that of the uplands as houses appear at much more frequent intervals.

At the road **G** turn right and follow this country lane with its flowery banks and overhanging trees. The valley to the right is attractive but not always peaceful as it is home to a rifle range. At the foot of the hill, just before the bridge, turn right onto the old railway line **H** – not our old friend this time, but a former Midland Railway branch line. The walk runs along the top of the embankment with a view down to the Wye, which is here indulging in one of its aimless meanders. The path leaves the railway via a stile, but continues to run beside it; you are now clear of the trees and the view opens out. The walk follows a rather uncomfortable line across the top of a very steeply sloping field below a wood, and then follows the edge of the wood downhill to a gate **I**.

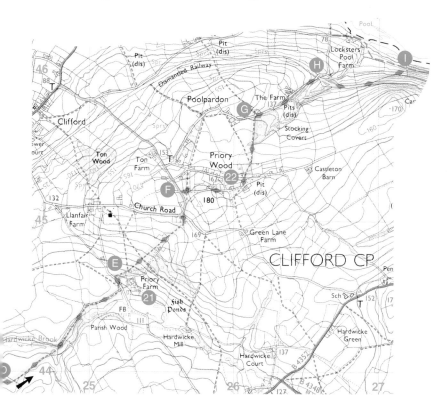

Rabbit
Bury
Wood

Rookery
Wood

Motte &
Bailey

River Wye (Afon Gwy)

Lower
Castleton
Farm

Old Castleton

Clock Mills

Upper
Castleton
Farm

Paddock
Farm

Cwmreel

Clock Mills
Bridge

St Oswald

PH

Green
Farm

Walnut
House

Waterfall

Orling
Castle

Middlewood
Bridge

Croft
Farm

Middlewood

Decry
Wood

Sydcombe
Farm

Newton Lane

West Brook

Newton
Farm

Newton Tump
Motte & Bailey

It then turns right and through the wood and becomes a good deal easier on a level path. As you leave the wood, the path and river are close together, but not for long: the river swings off one way and the path the other. There is a gentle uphill climb past an immense oak, its trunk ringed with fungus, to a rough hillside of gorse and bracken. At the fence by Rabbit Bury Wood where the path turns off to the left, turn right through the iron gate and head diagonally across the field to a wooden gate by the telegraph pole. At the road **J** turn left and stay with this lane as it winds round Lower Castleton Farm. Continue round to the left and as the lane climbs to the farm entrance turn left through the gate to take the path beside the hedge. There is a view down to the river, which is describing a great S through the fields. More importantly for the walker, the wooded slopes of Merbach Hill loom up ahead.

At a plantation of ornamental trees **23** turn away from the river up the driveway. The gardens to the left have beautiful trees and a cascaded stream. At the road **K** turn left to pass the ornamental gates to the estate and, just beyond the road junction, turn right onto the footpath signposted to Merbach. The path begins to climb, gently at first, between hedgerows. At the junction, continue straight on along the road marked 'No Through Road' and then almost immediately turn left on the track heading toward Merbach Hill. Where the path divides by a wooden gate **L** turn right and now the serious climbing

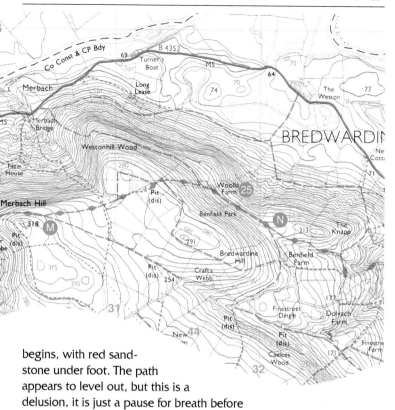

begins, with red sand-
stone under foot. The path
appears to level out, but this is a
delusion, it is just a pause for breath before
the next steep ascent. When the path eventually emerges above the
tree line **24** there is an immense view out over the river valley and the
surrounding hills. By the time you reach the summit you have topped
the thousand-foot (300-metre) mark and it feels like it!

The descent is particularly pleasant, and not just because it is going
downhill. There is an airy walk on a springy turf track through the
bracken. The obvious track turns right and is followed round for a few
yards and then turns left **M**.

Cross a stile, continue along the hedge and then follow the edge of
the wood, passing a large conifer plantation. Now there is a new view
of the wandering Wye. At the barn of Woolla Farm **25**, where the way
divides, continue down the hill, crossing over the track into the forest
and take the farm track heading downhill. Continue on the track
towards the farm, but before reaching it (count back two telegraph
poles from the farm) turn slightly left **N** to pass to the left of the farm
buildings. Continue on across the field, beyond the farm, and head to
the right of the cottage to join the road.

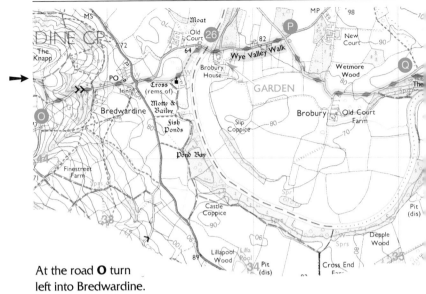

At the road **O** turn
left into Bredwardine.
Go straight on at the crossroads – though after
Merbach Hill many walkers may be tempted to pause at the pub. After
100 yards, turn right down the lane past the church and continue on
the footpath to return to the road by the delightful stone house, Old
Court **26** and it's turreted, romantic nineteenth-century neighbour. Turn
right to cross the Wye on a brick bridge, with a toll house at the end.
Brobury House on the far side is sufficiently grand to be able to open its
gardens to the public. Brobury Stud is rather curious: a stable block with
neat dormer windows. At the crossroads **P** turn right. There is a sign
announcing Neighbourhood Watch, though there is no obvious neighbourhood to watch. Everything now is very different from the earlier
part of the walk. With less readily available stone, houses are timber-
framed, producing the typical 'black-and-white' effect. The hills have
been left behind, and the hedgerows reveal another local speciality:
hops that have grown wild.

Where the dense woodland comes to an end on the right hand
side of the road **Q** turn right onto the path along the edge of the
wood and head into a dark tunnel of trees. There is no need to worry
about route-finding for a while, as the path scarcely deviates for the
next two miles. At first the wood is darkly impenetrable but soon
begins to open out and, for once, the dominant feature is not oak but
beech. This is a splendid wood of mature trees – there are names
carved on trunks a century ago. It is a magnificent sight with the trees
clinging to the steep bank and the gleam of the Wye far below. The

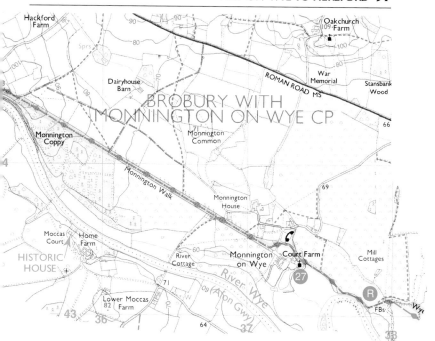

path remains at the upper edge of the wood. It is a pleasantly con-trasting walk, with the wood to one side and rich farmland to the other. Soon the path becomes a formal procession of trees, a stately avenue of green, Monnington Walk. The mixed woodland gives way to a large orchard and soon the tower of Monnington Church **27** appears at the focus of the avenue.

The walk finally deviates to the left round imposing Monnington Court and then turns back right towards St Mary's Church. Built in 1679, it is a plain but attractive building, notable for its many ornate monuments, some of which appear as carved stones set into the nave floor and one of which presents an interesting puzzle, being dated two years before the church was built. The path goes round the edge of the graveyard, turns left round a pond and then enters the Bulmer cider apple orchard. The orchard covers 127 hectares, and anyone who thought a cider apple tree was just a cider apple tree will soon find that they come in great variety of types, from little stumpy affairs to ones shaped like conifers. The walk follows the line of the hedge and halfway along it the Wye appears alongside. Beyond that, at an obvious break in the trees **R** by a bridleway sign, turn left through the orchard and leave it by a footbridge over a stream.

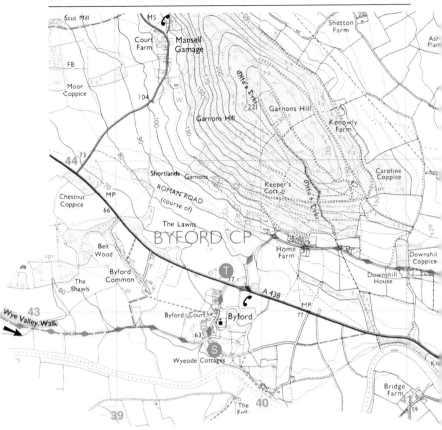

A clear, broad, grassy track through farmland continues alongside a row of poplars. Continue straight on along the bridleway to the road **S** and turn left into Byford, but it is worth pausing to look down to the right to a particularly handsome timber-framed house, the wood for once left in a natural state rather than painted black. Another timber-framed house shows the use of nogging, filling in the spaces between the timbers with rich, red brick. The road passes the church, with battlemented tower and the manor house to the side. At the road junction **T** turn right then left through the gates by a little Gothic lodge into typical, tree-dotted parkland. Follow the road round to the right towards the wooded hillside and continue on to the right at the woods. On one side are timber-framed houses on stone bases, one with a near-perfect cottage garden, and on the other Victorian red brick. The lane follows the line of a Roman road, and is so peaceful that you are more likely to

meet a wandering pheasant than a car. There is much to enjoy, from the birds twittering in the hedgerows to the wider views across the flat river valley to the Black Mountains. At the crossroads carry straight on through the linear village of Bishopstone, now overwhelmed by rather dull surburban housing. The view is now temporarily lost behind hedges, and the road continues in a straight line to the site of the old Roman town of *Magnis*, where it turns right, following the original town border. Here too is Lady Southampton's chapel, built, unusually in this area, of red brick. There is not much to see of *Magnis*, but the outline is still marked by lanes and field boundaries.

The road
comes down
to a willow-
fringed pond and bends
round to the right **U**. Here you turn off to the left onto
the footpath and follow it down to leave the fields by the gate
beside the cottage, from where a rough, gravel track leads
down to the main road **V**. Turn left at the road, and at the end of
the village, beyond the neat row of eighteenth-century brick cottages,
take the first turn on the right, signposted to Sugwas. It passes down an
avenue of mainly oak and horse chestnut, and up ahead is a long line of
poplars. They suggest a windbreak and, sure enough, an orchard has
been planted behind their shelter. New building materials appear in the
form of pantile roofs, and Sugwas Farm is notable for its exceptionally tall
chimneys. The road swings left past what was the Boat Inn and past
Wadworth Cottage, with a memorial to Horace Wadworth carved into
the gable. Here the road turns right **W**. Continue to the left down the

lane. Soon the tarmac gives way to a gravelled track, heading uphill at the edge of a wood. Cross the stile by the metal gate and take the path that turns right to follow the hedge. This is only a short climb, but it does provide an excellent vantage point from which to enjoy the scenery. Cross straight over the next field and continue on the farm track beside the orchard. Up ahead **28** is a very splendid timber-framed farmhouse with spectacular external chimneys. Turn right here onto the road and then, as the road bends **X**, turn left by the footpath sign, and climb the steps to a stile. Turn right round the edge of the field and along beside the wood to a stile in the far corner. The path now leads down to the road by Breinton House **29**. Turn right here, past the magnificent gateway topped by wrought-iron stags' heads. The road continues as a track down through the National Trust enclosure of Breinton Springs to the river. Turn left on to the riverbank **Y,** which will now be followed all the way to Hereford.

The river is broad and shallow here, running between sandy banks. Belmont House appears across the water, a fantastical creation of turrets, Gothic windows and decorative chimneys. The Walk now becomes quite busy, with anglers dotted along the river and golfers on the opposite bank hoping not to hear a plop of ball in water. Soon the water tower of Broomy Hill Waterworks **30** dominates the view. This is now a museum and can be visited by all with a passion for steam. The main exhibit is a superb triple-expansion pumping engine of 1895, which in its working days here pumped a million gallons of water in each twelve-hour shift. Just beyond the sports field is a handsome iron bridge that once carried a branch line that connected Hereford to the Mid-Wales rail system **31**. Its arrival marks the start of the walk through the outskirts of Hereford.

The old railway bridge across the Wye at Hereford now carries a cycle track as we

e Wye Valley Walk.

5 HEREFORD TO ROSS-ON-WYE

via Mordiford and Capler Camp   *16 miles (26 km)*

Cross over the railway bridge **31**, now used as part of a cycle track, and continue on down the riverbank towards Hereford city centre. From the old Wye Bridge **32,** which has now spanned the Wye for over five centuries, there is an enticing view of the cathedral. This alone makes an excursion into the city irresistible, if only for its superb chained library of 1444 volumes, with manuscripts dating back to the 8th century which are marvels of decoration. But for those who resist temptation or are returning to this point after an exploration, the Walk continues along the riverside into a park, where there are two monuments, a sad modest one to those who have drowned in the river and a triumphant column to Nelson. Cross over the elegant Victoria suspension bridge **33**.

Once over the river, turn immediately right onto the path behind the hospital, and then left round the

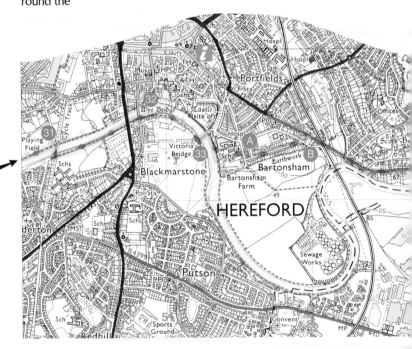

hospital grounds. Continue up the road past the school, with a row of almshouses on the right. At the junction **A** turn right and then immediately left down Park Street, an intriguing mixture of Victorian terraces and villas. At the T-junction **B** cross the road and turn right to go under the railway bridge – a rare encounter with an actual working line. There now follows what seems an interminable walk up the main road to get out of the suburbs, but there are things to look out for along the way. Opposite St Margaret's Road a handsome cast-iron milestone has survived, and many of the Victorian and Edwardian houses have a certain grandeur. Nevertheless, it is something of a relief when Sudbury Avenue **C** appears and the Walk turns off the road to the right and heads down to the river. There it joins the slow, placid stream and the Walk turns left along the bank. It is to be a short encounter. As the river begins to turn right by a solitary tree, turn left towards a causeway and flood bank, known unromantically as The Stank. Climb up the bank and follow the path along the top: an orchard has been planted, safe behind this protective earthwork. At the wooden gate **D** turn left down the steps to the road, turn right at the road and then left over the stile at the far end of the lay-by.

Head straight on, aiming for the path that runs beside the garden jutting out into the field, and take the path between the houses. At the road **E** turn left and follow the road as it turns sharply right and passes a little black and white cottage with a thatched roof and tiny windows peering out beneath reedy eyebrows.

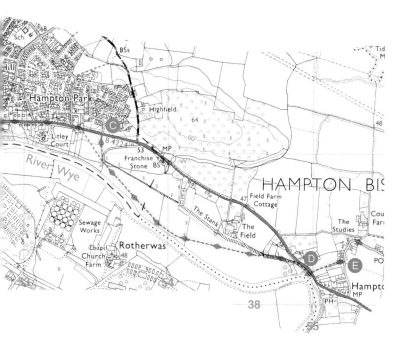

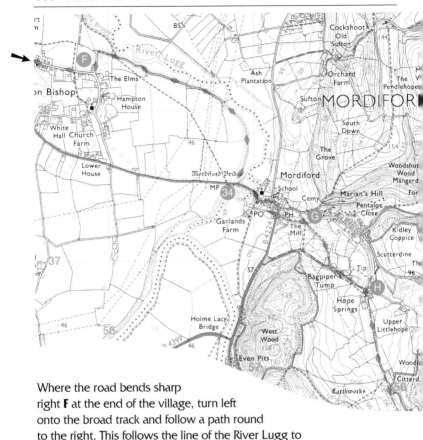

Where the road bends sharp
right **F** at the end of the village, turn left
onto the broad track and follow a path round
to the right. This follows the line of the River Lugg to
Mordiford. Incredibly, this little winding river was once navigable, and
in 1756 the seven bells of Leominster church were sent by barge all the
way to Chepstow for recasting. At the end of the track, turn left to cross
the old causeway and bridge **34** built in the fourteenth century and 'mod-
ernized' three hundred years ago. Below it are the remains of one of the
old flood gates that served as locks.

For a small place, Mordiford is full of delights, from the effortless
elegance of the Queen Anne house by the river to the homely church
with its Norman doorway and old rood screen. Follow the road up
through the village and round to the right, and immediately past the
mill **G** turn left onto the path up through the field. Cross a little stream
and go across the next field on a route parallel to the road. At the
next stile, turn through the orchard, keeping the hedge to the right,
and carry straight on along the lane bordered by hedges. Carry on in
the same direction on the surfaced road past Bagpiper's Cottage,

then as the road bends left **H** turn right through the farmyard up the obvious track. Where the track divides, keep straight on along the side of the field by the conifer plantation. The walk is now definitely heading back into hillier country, and the area is busy, but not with people. Rooks and pheasants conduct a noisy dialogue in the woods, and rabbits leap and run in every direction. The track peters out by a pair of metal gates, but the route continues in a straight line to cross a stile and then heads for the gap between a prominent clump of trees to the left and the woods to the right. Leave by the gate and take the track down to the road **I**.

Cross the road onto the track opposite which climbs up through the woods, first as a stony path then as a more defined farm track. Where the way divides, continue on as the track runs along the top of the ridge, with steep wooded slopes to either side; in summer, this is an area in which to look out for orchids. Where the path divides **J** turn half right along the footpath closed in by hedges for a short way, then turn off over a stile on the right. Follow the obvious path past a little strip of woodland, climb some wooden steps and turn left to a seat **35** and a splendid view of wooded hills, a glint of light from the river and more hills beyond. Continue through the wood and turn left over a stile to take the path down to the road. Cross straight over and continue on the path beside the wood, then follow it round into the Lea and Paget Woods, with more orchids to discover. Where tracks cross **K** turn right off the bridleway to leave the woods by the stile and continue along the path.

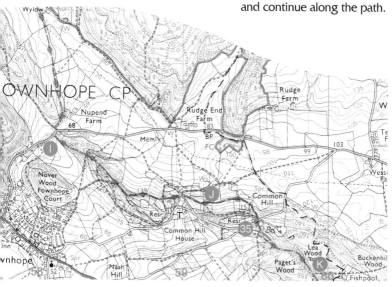

The Walk is now back into an area of mixed farmland, and heads down hill with a fence and hedge to the right. Beyond a metal gate, the path turns left to go round the edge of a field, right round the edge of the next field, then joins a farm track which is followed down to the road **L**. Turn left at the road, then immediately right onto the road signposted to Caplor Farm. Just before the barns, turn left over the stile to a field and then almost immediately right to find a stile tucked away in a corner. Beyond the farm, the track leaves the fields to become a little footpath on the fringe of the woods. This is now a steep climb, aided by wooden steps. At the top of these, follow the woodland round to the right and take the higher level path to emerge on the ramparts of Capler Camp **36**. This is a typical Iron Age hill fort: its builders made use of the natural defences of the steep hillside, then ringed the summit with a double bank and ditch. The walk runs down the ditch and continues into the edge of the wood, which teems with pheasants. Where the path divides **M** take the broad track that swings round a plantation of young trees towards an area of tall conifers. At the road, turn left at the picnic site, with a view down to the Wye **37** and then right. The track goes on, actually passing through the garden of West Cottage to another road crossing, to head diagonally right down a green lane. It makes a sharp turn to the left **N** still as a lane between hedges down to the road again **O**. This time, turn right onto the road.

Go straight on at the road junction to climb a little hill, but where the road turns sharp left, continue straight on along the path that heads for the woods, passing an old car and van that have been pressed into service as hen houses. At the foot of the hill, cross the stream and turn left. The stream provides pleasantly gurgling company for a time, as the path becomes a wider track that eventually ends at the road, by some notably prosperous looking houses **P**. Turn left, cross the bridge and turn right onto the path to rejoin the walk by the stream which soon hurries along down to the Wye. Turn left onto the riverside path.

The Wye has been something of a stranger for several miles, but now the path will stay with the river valley all the way to Ross. Unfortunately, the start of this section is a little frustrating. The path is a narrow strip at the edge of ploughed fields, and trees and tangled weeds stand between walker and water – even more annoyingly, one can see pleasant open grassy tracks on the other side. Happily it does not last, for a little bridge is crossed, and arable land gives way to grassland and a view across to a fishing lodge with an elaborate balcony. But this section is even shorter, for the path is forced away from

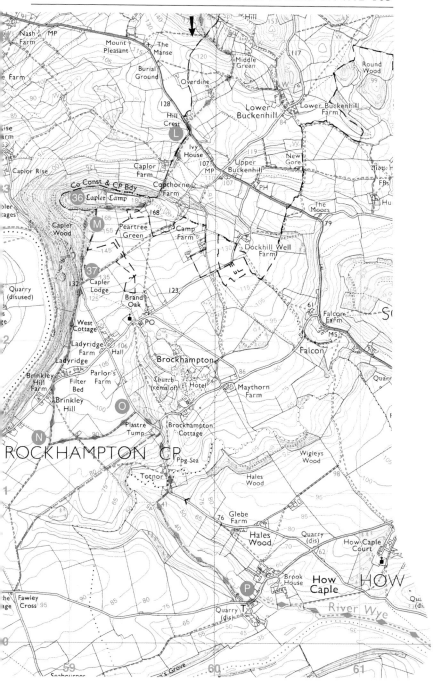

the river to join the road at the foot of a wooded hill. This is what one thinks of as typical Wye scenery, with woods piled high up above the winding river. The woods end at Hole-in-the-Wall, a youth adventure centre, where the Wye runs out of sight behind an island. When it reappears, by the Foy suspension bridge, the road shies away.

Just beyond Orchard Cottage **Q** turn right onto the footpath that cuts along the bottom of a plantation of densely planted spruce. When the wood ends, carry on along the path that approaches the farm track at a gentle angle. The fields leading down to the Wye have been stripped of fences and hedges, while the path runs along the foot of the hill. Where the field narrows down to a point, carry on along the bottom of the strip of woodland. From the wood the path heads towards the trees that line the riverbank. At the farm track **R** turn right. The river has looped up to this point and now goes away again, to pass between the piers of yet another disused railway **38**, this time one of the many branches of the Great Western system. The path and the river separate and the former heads off towards the obvious long, low railway embankment, which is followed for a way, until it is finally blocked off and the path joins the river at last.

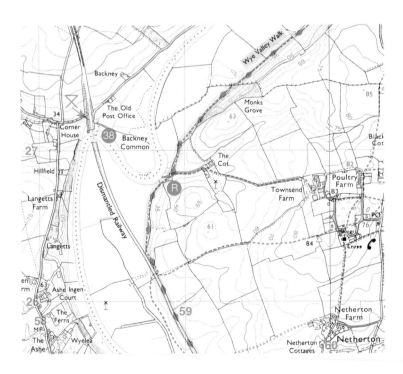

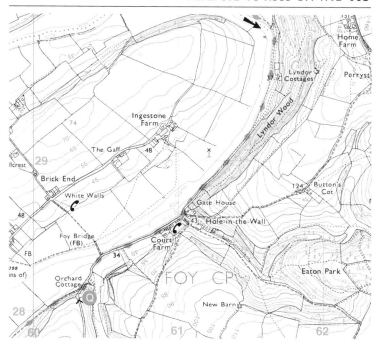

The old bridge across the Lugg at Mordiford.

The Walk heads under the modern road bridge carrying the busy A40(T). This is a little diversion away from the bank to cross a stream by a footbridge before the bank is rejoined. Over to the right Wilton Bridge **39** crosses the Wye, and Ross itself can be seen to occupy an airy perch above sandstone cliffs. Beyond the Riverside Restaurant, turn left and cross the driveway to go under the arches of the road to the car park at the edge of Ross.

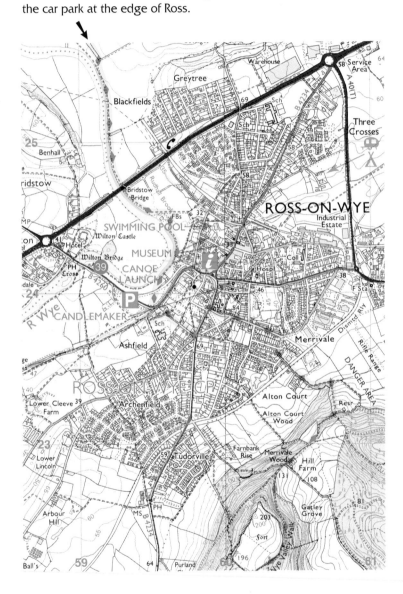

A distant view of Ross-on-Wye shows how the town clambers up the hillside above the river.

6 ROSS-ON-WYE TO MONMOUTH

via Kerne Bridge and Symonds Yat   *17 miles (27.5 km)*

The Wye Valley Walk seldom ventures far into the towns met along the way and Ross is no exception. That does not mean that it should be ignored, and the noble spire of the church certainly demands attention. Those who do explore will find at least one other memorable building, the market hall. Built in the reign of Charles II, it boasts a carving set there by the local philanthropist and Stuart supporter, John Kyrle, who also set out the Prospect Walk for the citizens.

It is this walk that the route now follows for a short way. Leave the car park by the footbridge next to the Wye Valley Walk notice board **A** and climb the wooden steps through a little wood. At the top of the steps, turn right, then almost immediately left through a kissing gate to take the path by the playing fields. At the roadway by Rectory Farm **B** turn right by the tennis courts and left onto the main road. After passing a Catholic church and an old thatched cottage that was originally a toll house, turn right along Alton Street **C**. The next right turn **D** down Penyard Lane begins, unpromisingly, at an industrial estate, but after crossing the old railway – and a goods wagon has found a home in a nearby field – the town is suddenly left behind.

The colonnaded market hall, Ross-on-Wye.

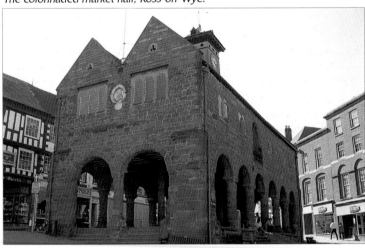

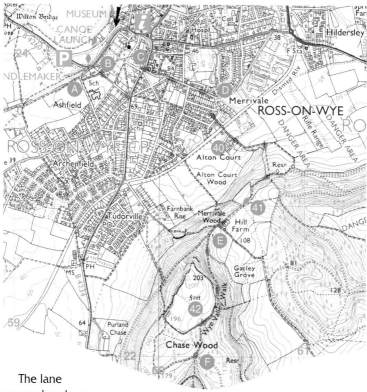

The lane passes handsome Alton Court **40** and then becomes a rougher track which swings uphill to run below the oak-dominated wood. A curious structure appears beside the path, a barrel-vaulted barn, which presents an urbane, pedimented façade to the grand house. The path swings round the edge of the wood, then passes through a narrow neck of woodland to continue following the edge of the wood to a clearing **41**. From here there is a view down to Ross and its dominant church. At the next stretch of woodland, turn right to cross a stile, then left by a memorial bench for the path heading through the wood. This emerges briefly by a farm and a track junction and continues straight on. Where the track divides by a wooden barrier **E** take the path on the left. There are extensive views out over wooded Penyard Park and to more distant hills. The path climbs steadily through Chase Wood, the site of another Iron Age hill fort **42,** but this one is not nearly so clearly defined as Capler Camp.

The track now levels out for a while, then divides **F**. Turn left, then immediately right off the broad track, onto a narrow footpath heading downhill. After a short way, the path splits again, and the route continues to the left on an ever steeper descent. Wooded steps ease the way through dense, tangled woodland. At the foot of the hill, follow the tongue of woodland round to the left and then go straight on down to the road **G**. At the road, turn left, and then, just before the road bends sharply to the left, turn right to follow a footpath on the other side of the hedge. Having just come down one hill, it is now time to go up the next. After crossing three stiles, there is a short, but very steep climb through a wild-looking wood, with massive boulders and beech trees spreading their branches overhead. The view opens out briefly at a small clearing **43** where the path turns left towards a stile at the left of a line of conifers. Arriving at a house, the path meets a broad track that at first levels out, then begins a gentle climb. Passing another cottage, take the path that goes steeply downhill.

Cross straight over the road **H** and continue on the downhill path along the edge of the wood then turn right to continue to the bottom of this deep, quiet valley. Now, of course, there is nothing for it but to climb up the other side. Go round the edge of the field to a stile on the right, climb the steps past the cottage to the road. Turn left, then immediately right onto the footpath signposted to Walford. Once again the path goes downhill, though by now experience suggests, quite rightly, that the easy progress will soon have to be paid for by another climb. But for the present, the narrow, shaded hollow way makes for pleasant walking and it soon emerges into the clear to continue the descent to the valley floor. The path crosses a house drive, and now the traffic which has been heard for some time can be seen on the minor road below. Path and road gradually merge, but as the road joins the river on its way

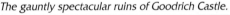
The gauntly spectacular ruins of Goodrich Castle.

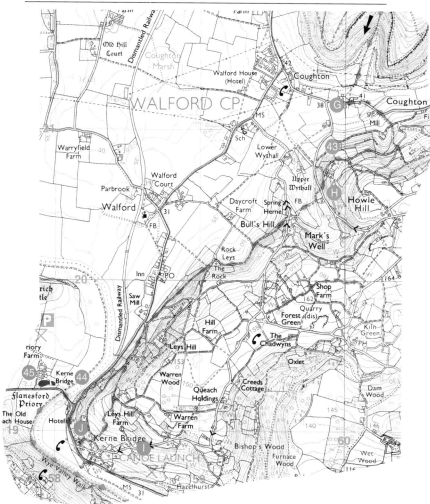

to Kerne Bridge, the path turns
away to put in one last hill before the river crossing.
This is a long steady climb on a sunken path that heads into a rocky,
woody landscape. Just before Leys Hill Farm **I** start to descend via a
track to the right. At the large house turn left down steps to meet the
main road at the Kerne Bridge Inn **J**. Cross straight over and turn right
onto the path beside the road and then turn left to cross Kerne Bridge
44. From here a short excursion can be made to Goodrich Castle (see
page 120) past Flanesford Priory **45**.

Once across the bridge, turn left to join the riverside path, and the
long ups and downs are over for a few miles. This is a particularly

grand sweep of river, rushing and swirling round the bend. A short flight of steps now leads up to an attractive woodland walk. The path soon dips down to the water's edge, passing through the abutments of yet another – and not the last – disused railway, this time an old Great Western branch line from Monmouth to Ross. Railway buffs will no doubt spot a length of old broad gauge track in use as a fence post. Just beyond the clearing, the line is joined for a while, before it disappears, originally going through a tunnel. The path takes an easier option, deserting the woodland for the water's edge. Across the river is a curious castellated tower beside a caravan park. There is not much space between woods and river, but just enough for the farmer to squeeze in an elongated field of grain. The woodland climbing up the hill makes a fine sight with the occasional tall fir piercing the mass of broad-leaved trees. The drumming of spotted woodpeckers can often be heard, and there is a good chance of a glimpse of the quieter green woodpecker. The path divides at the end of the woodland, but the route stays on the river bank. The Wye now goes into one of its convolutions, and it is clear from the swirl of hills that even more extravagant bends lie up ahead. The next obvious landmark, the tower of Welsh Bicknor church **47,** now appears up ahead, looking from here like a conventional tower in a jaunty party hat.

The river becomes quite agitated, dashing and gurgling round a stony islet. A certain amount of care is needed here, as inconsiderate rabbits

The lonely little church at Welsh Bicknor.

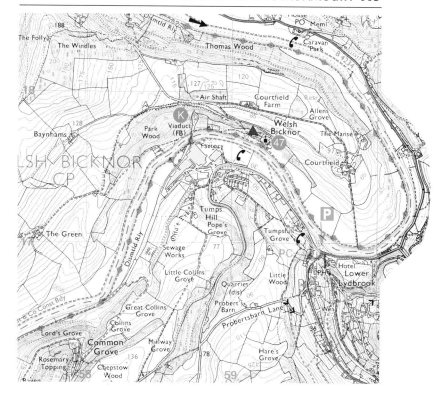

have dug their burrows right into, as well as around, the path. Excitement over, the river runs gently over shallows, streaming with weed, and the way opens up to a comfortable walk along grassy banks, the fields full of lolloping rabbits. Seen close to, the church tower is revealed as an Italianate campanile with a squat incongruous spire. More rabbits hop among the gravestones and round the ornate cross. Pass in front of the imposing house to join a broad riverside path, then turn right to join the railway re-emerging from its tunnel to cross the river on an iron viaduct **K**. Once on the bridge, the supports are seen to be hollow, riveted cylinders, and there is a chance to pause and enjoy the river scene, with sinuous green fronds reminiscent of a Monet painting.

Once over the bridge, continue on the riverside walk, signposted to Symonds Yat, passing a large redbrick packaging factory and a fishing lodge, the latter threatening the direst penalties to anyone who goes anywhere near it. Beyond the factory, the river is briefly lost to sight behind a screen of trees, but it soon opens out offering very pleasant walking over grassy fields. Then, however, as so often on the

A choice of boats at Symonds Yat: a leisurely cruise on a trip boat or a dash down

rby rapids by canoe.

Wye, the wooded slopes begin to creep ever closer to the water's edge and a shapely wooded cone soon blocks the way. An element new to the walk appears – stark grey cliffs of limestone thrusting vertically up from the trees. It is here, at Coldwell Rocks **48,** that the peregrines now breed. The path moves away from the river to cross a stile and enters the woods to climb a few steps to join the old railway. There is a hint of industrial activity in the region in the shape of lumps of shiny black slag from old copper works. The views become even more dramatic, with the river twisting and turning between the wooded slopes pierced by cliffs.

Just before the railway heads into the old tunnel **L** turn left onto the path signposted to Yat Rock. The path climbs steeply past the craggy cutting and a stone house, and then divides offering a choice of routes **M**. The shorter, but more energetic, goes in a direct line over the top of the hill, with the option of visiting the most famous viewpoint in the whole Wye valley, Yat Rock. The alternative goes in a long loop round the foot of Huntsham Hill.

As the former is much the more exciting, it will be described first. Take the uphill path by an old ruined forest boundary wall and climb up through a wilderness of pale beech, contrasting with mossy rocks and shiny green ferns. As the way steepens, the path is eased by zigzags and then by steps. It reaches a small cottage, then hairpins round and completes the climb up to the road, by a pair of old lime kilns. Cross straight over onto the footpath. This soon divides **N** with a branch to the left leading up to Yat Rock itself, a detour that is richly rewarded by the view **49**. The main walk goes straight downhill signposted to Symonds Yat East and Riverside. After a steep descent, it emerges from the wood past the Forest View Hotel and rejoins the river. Over to the right is The Saracen's Head and the hand-operated passenger ferry **50,** for anyone who wants to see the river on the opposite bank. It is here that the two routes unite.

Those opting for the long route turn right at **M** and take the path that gradually drops down to the edge of the wood to swing round the foot of the hill to the road. From this upper road it drops down to the lower road, and then turns right onto the footpath **O** that leads down to the river. The path now follows the river bank past another ferry serving the hotel on the opposite bank and on past The Saracen's Head. From here there are river cruises and boats for hire, including canoes. The walk now continues along the bank, passing a reach where a dashing set of rapids provides an interesting challenge and much excitement for novice canoeists. The railway is now joined again, this time passing through an avenue of trees. The rapids come to an end, the river

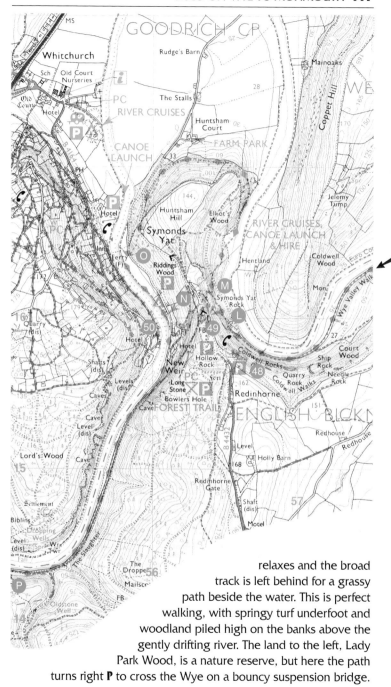

relaxes and the broad track is left behind for a grassy path beside the water. This is perfect walking, with springy turf underfoot and woodland piled high on the banks above the gently drifting river. The land to the left, Lady Park Wood, is a nature reserve, but here the path turns right **P** to cross the Wye on a bouncy suspension bridge.

Once over the bridge, turn left, not onto the obvious track, but onto the grassy path at the river's edge. Once again this is magnificent walking with, if anything, even more beautiful scenery. The river is still peaceful and tree-lined, but now there is the added dramatic effect of, first, boulders, then rocky outcrops and finally genuine crags. And the trees themselves are immense, some of the mighty beech being almost twenty feet in circumference, their tops lost from sight above the lower canopy of leaves. The path moves down to the water's edge and passes a forest lodge, surrounded by sycamores, which in autumn send their propeller seeds whirring down to your feet. The idyll, alas, is about to end. The path emerges into the open by an interesting castellated house with a huge array of greenhouses **Q,** but just beyond it is the busy A40 that will be a constant and noisy companion all the way to Monmouth. Fortunately there is still much to see and enjoy. An even grander house appears, with an unusual onion-domed turret, after which the river bends away and the woods again come down to the water, which keeps the cars out of sight if not out of earshot. A marker post is passed, informing walkers that they are leaving England and entering Wales. Beyond the woods the path continues to hug the riverbank and one is liable to find the water almost as busy as the roads with everything from rowing eights to canoeists. There is a mini diversion to cross a footbridge over a stream, after which the path passes through the churchyard of St Peter's Church **51**. Up ahead the far more impressive spire of Monmouth church appears in view. The walk passes a rowing club and arrives at the elegant Wye bridge and the road into Monmouth **52**.

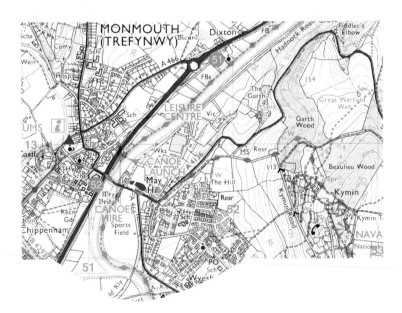

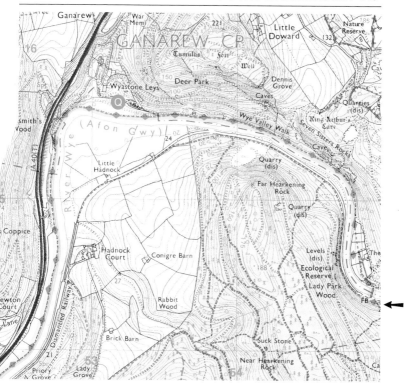

The picturesque scenery as the Wye makes its loop at Symonds Yat.

EXCURSION TO GOODRICH CASTLE

2 miles (3.2 km) return trip

From the west end of Kerne Bridge **44** carry straight on up the road past Flanesford Priory **45**. The Augustinian house was founded in 1346, but all that remains is the splendid refectory of red sandstone with Decorated windows, now converted to a private house. Continue up the road under the impressive arch of the railway viaduct, then turn right at the crossroads **A** into Goodrich village, where there is also an inn for those who want to combine the visit with a longer break. Turn immediately right beyond the crossroads for the road to the castle.

At the car park **B** carry on along the track with a fine beech-wood hanger to the left and extensive views over the Wye to the right. It is easy to see the strategic importance of the castle on its lofty perch overlooking an ancient crossing of the Wye. Over the river is Walford or Welsh Ford, and the Roman road from Gloucester to Caerleon probably crossed nearby as well. The castle itself **46** has a formidable appearance and seems to have grown out of the rocks on which it stands. The most imposing features are the round towers standing on square bases, with spurs as buttresses. The entrance itself is via the barbican, which originally involved crossing two bridges over the moat, a daunting prospect for an attacker. There is a charge to go inside, but the visit is very much worthwhile. The same route is then followed back to the main walk.

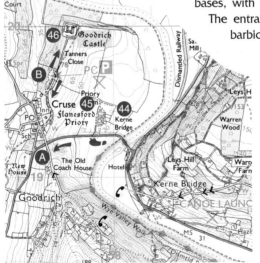

The walls of Goodrich castle, built out of the same red sandstone on which the fortress stands.

Circular walk to The Kymin

2½ miles (4 km)

The walk starts at the eastern end of Wye Bridge **52**. Carry on up the main road and take the A4136 to the left past the Mayhill Hotel **A** on your right. Cross over the road and continue up the hill for a short way, then take the footpath that slides away into the woods on the right, signposted Offa's Dyke Path. The path soon begins a steady climb through the trees to emerge on a quiet lane, bounded by hedges. Just beyond the reservoir **B** where the road turns sharply right, cross the stile and take the path straight ahead through the woods. There is a stiff climb through dense woodland which eventually opens out, and the way becomes a little easier. At the top of this hill **C** turn right to cross a stile on the edge of the field, then follow the path round the wood to the left towards a telecommunications tower. The next landmark is a stile by a house, which leads to the road. Turn left and immediately turn off again for another climb through woods. At first it is a typical, dense, dark conifer plantation, but soon changes to boulder-strewn broad-leaved woodland. A steep climb leads to a massive beech tree, where the path turns left. Stone steps lead up a

The Kymin Round House looks down over Monmouth.

122

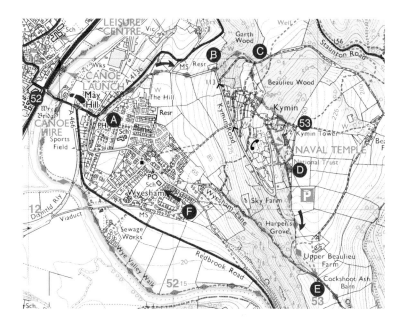

rock face which is then passed to the right before you finally emerge at the top of the hill.

In front of the delightful castellated cottage, Kymin Tower **53**, seats provide an opportunity to recover from the climb and take in the breathtaking panorama of Monmouth and the valley. The path now goes on to the little classical Naval Temple, built in 1800 with Britannia perched on top the inscribed names of 'noble admirals who distinguished themselves by their glorious victories for England'. Carry on to the car park and leave by the road. As it begins to turn downhill **D** turn left through a kissing gate onto the footpath sign-posted to Upper Redbrook. The enclosed path soon opens out to fields on the left and heads steadily downhill along the edge of the wood, with more superb views to enjoy. Cross a stile in the fence on the right by a converted stone barn **E** and double right back onto the grassy track heading into the wood. As the path heads downhill, the scrubby areas give way to more mature woodland, and it becomes more of a recognized forest road, with old tumbledown stone walls to the side. Go straight on until the first houses appear and continue on along the roughly surfaced road. Turn right on to the road **F** and stay with it past a school and a church. The houses become more scattered, spaced by fields, and the main road is reached by the Mayhill Hotel. Return to the start.

7 MONMOUTH TO CHEPSTOW

via Redbrook and Tintern   *17 miles (27 km)*

The official walk once again misses out the town – and again there is much to enjoy. Agincourt Square has statues of two local heroes: Henry V looking down, literally if not metaphorically, upon the Hon. C. S. Rolls of Rolls-Royce and early aviation fame, and the Monnow is crossed by a unique fortified bridge **54**. Nelson was a freeman of the town, and as well as being commemorated by a collection in the museum, he is honoured with other naval heroes at the Kymin, which is visited as part of a circular walk (see page 122).

The Wye Valley Walk crosses over the bridge **52**, before turning right to run along the edge of the sports fields by the river. It passes two railway viaducts **55**, both disused. The first is an iron design of the kind already met, but the other is a far more impressive affair in stone. The river section has been demolished, but the rest stretches away across the fields on a long procession of arches. A narrow path wriggles past an aromatic sewage works, but once that is gone the beauty of the Wye reasserts itself in what is now a familiar, but never boring, pattern. Fields spread out from the path to a background of clumpy hills. Stiles along the route now stand in farcical isolation, for the fences have all gone and the area between road and river is now virtually one huge field. Woods alternate across the river; as the trees creep up to line one bank, they recede from the other. There is a little, twisty, stony section through trees, then the path re-emerges into fields, with the road now very close at hand, until at the edge of Redbrook **A** path and road merge. It is a short conjunction. At the houses, the path turns off to the right and runs past the football field. This area was the site of a copper works until 1771, when it was converted to tinplate rolling, remaining active right up to 1962. Turn right again at the river bank to cross a railway viaduct **B** in the familiar style.

This is a lovely stretch of river, especially on a still day, when the trees are reflected in the calm waters. At the far end is the Boat Inn, which was once the site of a ferry. Continue up the lane for a short way, then turn left onto the railway track bed which will be followed for the next couple of miles. This time we have arrived at the Wye Valley Railway, which must have been an absolute delight before its working days were ended in 1959. Views constantly open up down

to the river, here lined with small fishing lodges, while the hillside trees must almost have brushed the carriage windows. Extra interest is provided by the strip of grassland by the river, just wide enough to allow space for a few cattle to graze.

At the end of the wood **C** turn right onto the road past Tump Farm with the White Brook gurgling away to the right. Soon the first tumbledown buildings of the paper mills that used the stream to turn their water wheels appear on the right, and there are more extensive remains by the house **56**. A few yards beyond this, turn left off the road onto the footpath for the start of what will be a long climb right up to the rim of the narrow Wye valley. The path turns back at an angle to the road, and soon provides a view down the beautiful Whitebrook Valley with its handsome houses. It climbs steeply between stone walls and massive boulders, and where it divides by a broad track just keep straight on up the hill. When a little flight of stone steps is met, do not go up them but turn left for what becomes something of a corkscrew progress uphill. Just as it is all starting to feel remote and wild, houses are met **D**. Turn left onto the road, still inexorably climbing. At the top of the hill, as the slope begins to ease, views open out over the valley. There is another short climb, and someone has taken pity on the walker and provided a bench at the edge of a green. Where the road doubles back round the green turn left onto the broad track. After a while the surface becomes rougher, and where the way divides by a holly hedge turn right uphill once again. This path comes out on another road **E**. Turn left and now the top of the hill really has arrived at last. Where the road divides carry straight on down a lane bordered by hedgerows which reaches a dead end at a wooden gate **F**. The directions for reaching this point may have sounded complex, and the maze of paths seen on the map looks daunting, but in practice there are no real problems, and route-finding now becomes very much easier.

Beyond the gate, the track leads through woodland at the rim of the valley, and from here one can see just what a serpentine course the Wye has carved through the hills. An area of pine proves very attractive to green woodpeckers, and then the track heads into an area of new and mature conifer plantations. Beyond this point, at a meeting of tracks **G** take the narrow path ahead that begins to go downhill. This is a particularly pleasant walk on a sandy, stony path, dappled by sunlight filtered through the trees. The rough hillside is dotted with boulders and crossed by an old moss-covered boundary wall. At a clearing by a house, a splendid view right down to the river pops up unexpectedly **57**.

At the road **H** carry straight on along the track opposite, crossing what is a bounding stream in wet weather but may be a dry rocky gully at other times. The walk changes character again, now there is open farmland to one side and tall firs to the other. At the track junction take the middle way, signposted to Bargain Wood. There is a view of the hills across the valley. After about 300 yards turn left **I** on to a broad track. Now there are even wider prospects of wooded hills up ahead and glimpses of rich farmland. A number of seats along the way offer an opportunity to relax and enjoy the views. The track swings round to the right and ends at a picnic area **58**. Carry on towards the car park, then, just before the road is reached, turn left onto the path that crosses a stream.

The narrow path winds through a wood which echoes with the squawks of jays. After passing through a smaller picnic area surrounded by pine, the path heads into a denser conifer region, offering silent walking on a soft cushion of pine needles. Where tracks meet, turn right **J** on to a rocky path, and then turn immediately right again to head down to the road. Turn left at the road and almost immediately, as the road begins to bend, turn right to head back into the woods. Cross over the wide forest road and continue on the path that winds through what is now mainly broad-leaved woodland. The Walk emerges at a clearing, with a flagpole, used as a scout camp.

The old Ferry Boat inn at Redbrook.

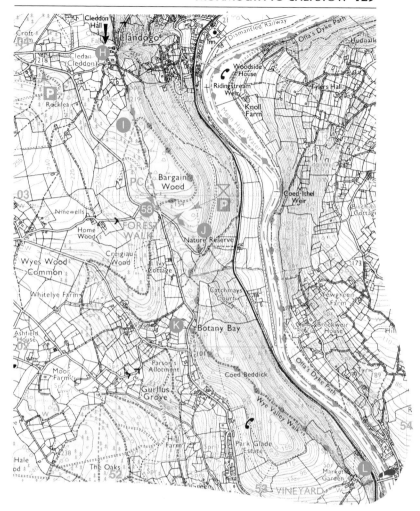

Upon reaching the roadway **K** turn left by a small pond
and, once past the house, turn left again, back into the woods. It is a
little disconcerting to find oneself climbing uphill again, but the path
soon levels off and then starts to descend. This is a somewhat disori-
entating though attractive route through the woods, and it is with
some relief that one glimpses the hills across the Wye, a reassurance
that one really is going in the right direction. Reaching the valley rim,
the way steepens as it goes down through an area of coppiced woodland. Where the way divides, take the path on the left down wooden
steps that hairpin their way down to the road **L**.

Cross over the road and turn right towards Brockweir Bridge, which is the starting point for a circular walk up to Offa's Dyke and The Devil's Pulpit (see page 136). Just before the bridge, go down the steps and turn right to join the old Wye Valley Railway for the last, and most interesting, encounter. The Wye itself has changed a good deal since we last met it: the sparkling water and sandy banks have gone, to be replaced by a turbulent, muddy, tidal river that leaves the banks gleaming like chocolate icing. The track now arrives at Tintern Old Station **59,** complete with signals and signal box, platform, waiting room and old coaches. It now serves as picnic area, café and information centre, with displays on the history of the line. The only trains that run, however, are miniature ones, dwarfed by their full-scale neighbours. The track bed is followed to the river; here there is a yawning gap where a viaduct once stood. Turn right down steps to the riverside walk. There are notices warning against bathing – though one cannot imagine anyone wanting to plunge into that brown, fast-flowing stream. The path goes through the churchyard of the parish church **60**. There has been a church here since 765, but the plain, simple church we now see was largely the result of a Victorian rebuild, though a fine medieval font remains. From here the path goes up to the road and turns left.

The Walk now stays with the footpath by the main road through Tintern, and soon the famous abbey itself **61** comes into view. But just before it is reached there is an area that was once the scene of furious industrial activity. What is now the Royal George Hotel was originally home to the owner of the Tintern Wireworks. The pond provided power for the water wheels that worked the forge. The stone building across the road was part of the complex, later adapted for use as a corn mill and wood turnery. A short railway ran across the girder bridge, now a footbridge, linking it to the Wye Valley line. Many walkers will want to carry on along the road to visit the abbey, but the Walk itself turns off to the left on the first turning past the hotel **M** onto a minor road that runs away at a shallow angle. Once past the houses there is a good view of the abbey. This road eventually peters out and continues as a track bordered by stone walls.

This is the start of the last long climb of over 700 feet (230 metres) to the top of the hills above the Wye. It is a dark and gloomy way, closely hemmed in by lowering and gloomy forest. Soon rocks appear on either side and the path climbs up a natural staircase of stone. There is a respite as the track levels out, it then turns left **N** to cross a stream and go up a little flight of steps before continuing to the left. Leave the wood by the stile for a meadow, splashed with the yellow of buttercups and fleabane. Make for the telegraph pole and then for a stile at

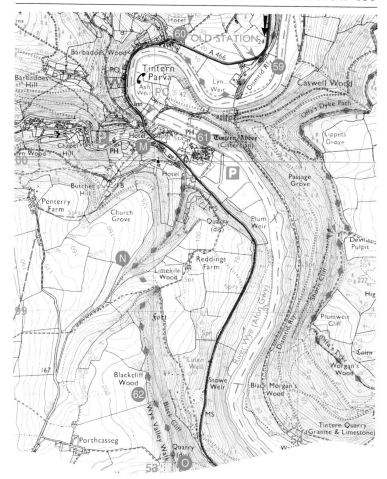

the edge of the wood. Once over that, turn right on the path that again climbs up between the trees, then swings to the right for a while, only to turn left for a much steeper climb to a little rocky wilderness, once the site of a small hill fort. The path becomes rather indistinct but still heads, if rather more gently, uphill. It then goes through a zigzag, almost a scramble, and at last the ground ahead can be seen falling instead of rising. The top of the hill has finally arrived **62**.

The path now turns left to run along the top of the steep valley side, into an area of dark woodland where rocks and gnarled roots lay snares for the careless. Having got one's breath back, it is now easier to enjoy the woodland walk. After a while, another path is reached **O**.

Turn right and then left to carry on in the same general direction, but now with glimpses of farmland over to the right as the path continues along the fringe of the wood. A little footpath on the left provides a short diversion to The Eagle's Nest **63**, a viewpoint as spectacular as Yat Rock. The path comes back up to the main walk, which now heads steadily downhill. At the edge of the field **64** there is a hairpin bend with a view down to the Severn and its two immense road bridges. The path comes out at a car park **P**, goes straight on along the road, then doubles back on a footpath that heads very steeply downhill. It then becomes a grassy track that emerges at another road beside a quarry **Q**. Turn right down the road to the car park and turn left onto the broad obvious, track that runs away at a slight angle to the road.

The next section of Walk was one of the most famous of the picturesque walks above the Wye, and as if nature had not provided drama enough, man added his own artificial wonders. At first it is a narrow, twisting way that clings to a narrow hillside ledge, with scrambles over and between rocks. Where the view opens out, towering limestone cliffs can be seen rearing up above the river. Then the path plunges into a dark tunnel through the rocks, beyond which is a tiny artificial grotto **65**. Down below, the Wye can be seen going through its last major convolution, while the Walk takes a short cut across the promontory. It passes through an area of coppicing and, just beyond an old kiln, it throws in one last climb. The path swings round the head of a steep-sided valley, and arrives at a fence and one more brilliant viewpoint, this time down to Chepstow Castle **66** in its magnificent site above the river.

Beyond the viewpoint, turn left through a gap in the stone wall to take a path that runs down past a school to the road **R**. Turn left to head down into Chepstow, passing a very grand house on the right. The Walk does not just fizzle out in town streets – if you turn left off the road **S** into the park, the path then leads to a truly magnificent finale at the walls of Chepstow Castle.

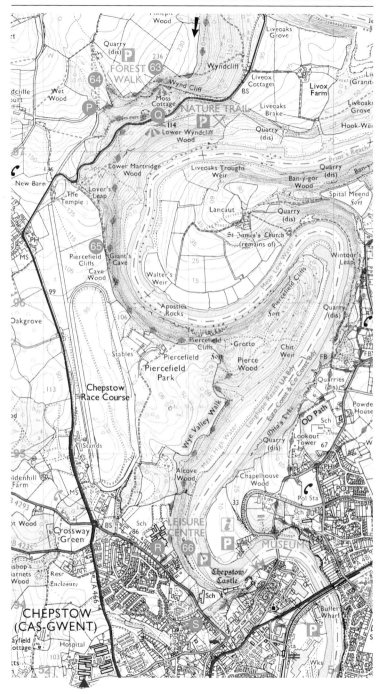

Nearing Chepstow, the walk takes a high level route, with panoramic views over t